The Game Isn't Everything

The Game Isn't Everything
The Reality Beyond the Arena

I would have loved to win a Pulitzer, but being a friend of someone who won it is quite enough for me.

With affection more than envy,

Bruce Lowitt

November 2018

By BRUCE LOWITT

ISBN-13: 978-1534981126 (CreateSpace-Assigned)
ISBN-10: 1534981128

Barstad Communications
CoBia imprint

To Arlene, Stephanie and Adam,
who have given me the best of my life.

Table of Contents

Private Lives was a weekly personal essay column that appeared in the St. Petersburg Times, succinct works of nonfiction submitted by professional and amateur writers.

Acknowledgements

My profound thanks to Dave Klein, Dave Gussow, Hal Bock, Don Harrison, Marty Appel, Kate Sullivan, Mike Harris, Jack Stephenson, Marc Topkin, Warren Randall, David Bernstein, Karen Dawkins, Charles Einstein, Thomas C. Tobin, Harry Atkins, Dan Berger, Duke Maas, Terry Taylor, Mike Stephenson, Kitty Bennett, Darrell Christian, Murray Rose, and Ron Peal, some of whom are no longer with us, but all of whom have had an impact, whether major, slight or somewhere in between, on the success I have experienced in my chosen career.

But most of all, to Mr. K.

Dedication

Mr. K.

It was early 1957 and I was, as usual, in the back row of my sophomore history class. Unless ordered otherwise, I was by choice in the back row of every class in high school – and, as usual, my mind was elsewhere.

I was engrossed in a MAD Magazine when a large hand grabbed it away and a low voice rumbled, "See me after class, Mr. Lowitt." I'd been caught dead to rights by Mr. K.

Andrew Kuchinsky was a bear of a man. Not fat, just big, with a broad chest and big shoulders. He got his B.A. and M.A. from Columbia University so he must have been pretty smart.

And he was chairman of the History Department at Adelphi Academy in Brooklyn, the prep school I attended.

Mr. K. never shouted out names to get our attention. Instead, he would take a pinkie-sized piece of blackboard chalk and fire it unerringly at a student whose behavior displeased him. It would leave a *gotcha* on a jacket or blouse, and trying to brush the splash of white powder to invisibility was futile.

As ordered, I stopped by his desk after class. He was seated and the MAD Magazine was lying face down, partly hidden under some papers. Not even trying to explain my conduct, I said, "Sir?"

He opened a desk drawer, picked up the comic book, and dropped it in, then closed the drawer, began writing some sort of note and, without looking up, said, "Pick it up at the end of the semester."

"Yes, sir," I said and began to turn away.

Mr. K. looked at me and said, "Mr. Lowitt, I'm keeping an eye on you."

It was ominous. Half of the semester remained, and two years after that. I was, at best, a mediocre student. A lot of times I found myself daydreaming in class or trying in vain to concentrate on what the teacher was saying.

My retention was terrible. Homework was a nightly trial. I would overhear my father tell my mother that I'd probably never amount to much.

It would be many years later before anyone identified Attention Deficit Disorder.

And now Mr. K. was going to keep an eye on me. I vowed to do better in his class. A lot better.

My year-end grade was a C, no different from my freshman year. I reported to Mr. K. after the final class. He opened his briefcase, pulled out the MAD Magazine and handed it to me, then told me to sit, took a chair opposite mine, and asked me about my goals.

I had none, so I blurted out that I wanted to be a teacher. He said nothing, so I said, "I …"

Mr. K. interrupted me. "Mr. Lowitt, I don't know why you don't pay attention in class. I don't know why you can't finish your home-work. You'll probably figure it out some day. I don't know what's going on in that mind of yours. But I can tell you this …" He looked hard into my eyes. "Bruce, you're better than you think you are."

Silence, then, "You're free to go. But remember what I just told you. You are better than you think you are. Trust me."

I graduated - barely - two years later, spent a couple of years in college where I wrote for the fraternity newspaper, and got a few jobs over the next three years – proofreader for a printing company, researcher at the Securities and Exchange Commission, copy editor for Moody's Investors Service.

I thought sparingly about Mr. K., maybe a few times a year when I was particularly depressed about my job, my lack of height, my surplus weight, the absence of a social life.

I was supposed to be better than this. He'd told me I was better.

I would try for a while. Sometimes the effort bolstered my self-esteem for the rest of the day.

By then it was 1965. I was 23. I had discovered Jimmy Breslin's columns in the New York *Herald Tribune* and I fantasized about being a newspaperman. Then I decided to go for it.

After months of interviews and rejections I was hired by a suburban New York City afternoon paper, the Port Chester *Daily Item*, in a blue-collar community. I left a year and a half later, in 1967, when The Associated Press hired me.

I stayed with The AP for 19 years, mostly as a sports writer in Los Angeles and New York, then joined the St. Petersburg Times in 1986, where I covered sports for 17 years before retiring from fulltime writing in 2004.

It was at the 1996 Atlanta Olympics when, for the first time in years, I suddenly thought about Mr. K.

I sat frozen, hearing his words. I was better than I'd thought I was. I was doing what I wanted to do and doing it well, and I was getting paid to do it.

I had to tell him he'd been right all along. I grabbed the phone, called Adelphi Academy and asked if Andrew Kuchinsky was still teaching there.

No, the voice in Brooklyn said. He had retired a number of years ago and had died that February, just five months earlier.

I wept at the thought that Mr. K. never knew how I had turned out, and that I'd never thanked him.

Introduction

I was 17 when I first saw -30-, a 1959 film about a day in the life of a fictional Los Angeles newspaper. Looking back at it now, it is trite, with obvious plots and subplots, and clichés for everyone in the newsroom – a sarcastic city editor, nerd science writer, grande dame society writer and so on, and steely night editor Jack Webb, who also produced and directed it.

There is a scene, though, in which city editor Jim Bathgate (William Conrad), holding a rolled-up newspaper and smacking it into his palm after each sentence for emphasis, is chewing out a copyboy, who is denigrating the newspaper business and talking about quitting:

"Do you know what people use these for? They roll them up and they swat their puppies for wetting on the rug! They spread them on the floor when they're painting the walls! They wrap fish in them! They shred them up and pack their two-bit china in them when they move, or else they pile up in the garage until an inspector declares them a fire hazard!

"But this also happens to be a couple of more things. It's got print on it that tells stories that hundreds of good men all over the world have broken their backs to get. It gives a lot of information to a lot of people who wouldn't have known about these things if we hadn't taken the trouble to tell them. It's the sum total of a lot of guys who don't quit.

"*Yeah, it's a newspaper, that's all. Well, for once you're right, stupid! It only costs ten cents, that's all. But if you only read the comic section or the want ads it's still the best buy for your money in the world.*"

That speech first inspired me to even consider life as a newspaper reporter.

One

One last chance

TAMPA - One by one, his chances turned to dust. Like a pitcher grooving one fastball after another, hanging one curve after another, he watched them disintegrate until there was nothing left for him but a trip to the showers. Or oblivion.

Steve Howe is 33 now, making the latest and probably last comeback of a Major League career that has wound through Los Angeles, through Minnesota and Texas and through a mountain of cocaine and a river of alcohol.

Today he wears the pinstripes of the New York Yankees, hoping to hook on as the replacement for Dave Righetti. His chances are good. A left-handed relief pitcher, even a troubled or potentially troublesome one, is a rare commodity when his fastball is clocked at 92 mph.

"I'm as strong and as mentally fit as ever," Howe said, "probably better than before, because I don't put chemicals into my body. My eyesight hasn't gone. My kidneys, my liver, my heart, they're in great shape."

But if the fates or his own temptation conspire against him again, if he never pitches another Major League inning, well, he says, it wouldn't be the end of the world.

1

It wasn't always thus. There was a time, he said, "when the sole existence of what I did in life, the only thing that defined me, was what I did on a ballfield. I used to let everyone else's thoughts run my life. I did drugs for me. I didn't like to feel the way I felt. Drugs turned off that feeling. Even if it turned it off for five minutes, it was better than where I was at that time.

"My world was safe when I was playing baseball, and when the chemicals took hold and I couldn't get to the stadium, I couldn't be where I was safe. So my world came tumbling down rather quickly."

Howe last pitched in the majors in 1987. He has been suspended six times for drug and alcohol abuse. He said he hasn't touched either for more than two years - since Jan. 22, 1989, to be exact.

"Our mental well-being comes as we get priorities straight," Howe said. "Before, my career was up front. Nothing else, nobody else, mattered. Today, family and God are most important to me. Baseball - my career, whatever it is - is secondary.

"I'll put my marriage and family life up against anybody's in the world. That's all I want, a healthy family, healthy kids, a healthy relationship with my wife. Anything else is cake. Right now, I'm experiencing some cake."

"You know what I think Steven's problem was?" his mother, Barbara, said. "Everything he ever said he wanted to do, he did. He's an ordinary kid who got everything he ever wished for. All his dreams came true. And it wasn't enough."

Virgil Howe was 16 and Barbara 15 when Steve, the first of their five children, was born. "Kids bringing up kids is what it was," Steve said. They both worked for General Motors.

They have since retired and moved from Detroit to a community off Lake Michigan. Their four other children all work and live in Michigan - Jeffrey a heavy equipment operator, Michael in heating and cooling, Kathleen with GM, and Christopher in the hardwood floor business.

Steve was the star athlete in the family - all-state in high school, all-Big Ten twice at the University of Michigan, National League Rookie of the Year for the Dodgers in 1980, a world champion in 1981.

"When he was 9, he said he was going to play Major League baseball," his mother said. "When he was a kid, whatever he said he was going to do, it came easy. And once he got it, it was always, 'This isn't what I really want.' "

Steve and Cyndy Howe married in June 1979, the same month the Dodgers made him their No. 1 selection in the free-agent draft. He spent that season in San Antonio, their Class AA farm team, before riding his 94-mph fastball to The Show.

Baseball, he said, was what gave him his self-esteem.

"Inside, I didn't feel good about myself," Howe said. "That's a character defect. There's no reason why I had it. I just had it. Call it alcoholism, call it dysfunction, whatever you want. There was a false pride, an arrogance that was destructive. I didn't appreciate what I had because I didn't feel I deserved it, and at the same time I felt everybody owed it to me. I was caught in that middle ground."

A rich young star, even a newly married one, doesn't automatically settle down in the suburbs. Howe didn't. He and Cyndy roared into Marina del Rey, the freeway off-ramp to the California fast lane.

He was invited into the celebrity circle - movie stars, power-brokers. He was 22 and very much sought after in a world and an era where cocaine was the fun thing to do, just another toy of the super-rich.

"I never knew he was taking it," said Tommy Lasorda, the Dodgers' manager then and now. "But I'd caution him, 'I don't know who you're hanging around with, but remember one thing; if you sleep with dogs, you wind up with fleas. Be careful.' He'd say, 'I know, I know. You're right,' and then he'd go do it anyway."

By the end of 1982, Howe's third season, cocaine had become such a part of his life he spent 5½ weeks at a clinic in the Arizona desert.

On May 23, 1983, Chelsie Leigh Howe was born. At the time, her father was finishing the first of six weeks of drug-abuse treatment at a hospital in Orange, Calif.

Steve Howe was suspended by the Dodgers for one day in July 1983 after he showed up three hours late for a game against Chicago, then was suspended again for the rest of the season on Sept. 23. On Dec. 15, 1983, then-commissioner Bowie Kuhn suspended him for the entire 1984 season. A week later, the Howes, owing about $100,000 more than they had, filed for bankruptcy.

Howe underwent more counseling and rehabilitation in 1984. The Dodgers gave him a one-year contract for 1985.

At spring training, Al Campanis, then the Dodgers' vice president of player personnel, approached Howe. He had read it was dangerous for an addict to use any other kind of chemical substance, that even smoking could lead to a relapse. Howe smoked.

He offered Howe a deal. They would set up a fund for Chelsie. For every day Howe abstained, Campanis would put in a dollar. For every day he smoked, Howe would kick in two. It was run on the honor system - but occasionally Campanis would walk up to Howe and say, "Breathe on me."

As Opening Day approached, Howe announced: "Drugs are right where they belong, in the past."

On June 23, 1985, he showed up three hours late for a game against Houston. One week later, he failed to show up for a game against Atlanta.

On July 3, Howe asked the Dodgers to release him. "I had sports writers hiding in my backyard, following my wife around the grocery store," he said. "Things had gotten out of hand." The Dodgers released Howe.

He was still smoking.

On Aug. 11, the Minnesota Twins signed him. On Sept. 12, Howe appeared on the ABC program Nightline. Cocaine, he said, was not his problem. It was life itself. Three days later, he vanished. And three days after that, he reappeared, met with Twins officials, asked for and was given his unconditional release. He entered rehabilitation in Minneapolis.

On Aug. 6, 1987, Texas signed him. On Jan. 17, 1988, after he had violated his after-care program by using alcohol, the Rangers released him.

No team would touch him, but he couldn't let go.

In January 1990, Howe applied for reinstatement. Commissioner Fay Vincent gave his consent - providing Howe could prove himself with a year in the minors. Howe spent the 1990 season with Salinas of the Class A California League, then played winter ball with Mazatlan of the Mexican League.

Last Feb. 21, the Yankees were granted permission to sign him. If he makes the roster, he will earn a minimum $100,000. He figures that, without his episodic use of alcohol and drugs over an eight-year stretch, he might have made as much as $10-million. It is not that far-fetched, considering more than 200 major-leaguers receive $1-million-a year or more.

Howe said he just wants to make enough to spend his life fishing and watching his kids grow up. "If I can't," he said, "I can make a buck elsewhere. Like in counseling for alcohol and drug abuse."

As part of his agreement with the Yankees, Howe says he will submit to periodic drug testing.

"When Steven was growing up," Barbara Howe said, "he messed up so seldom that when he did, and got reprimanded for it, it was a real big deal to him. He didn't like to take the blame for doing something wrong."

Chelsie Howe is almost 8 now. Her brother Brian turns 4 in June.

Steve Howe said Chelsie knew when she was about 4 that her father was a drug addict. "We'd discuss that stuff with her all the time. We do it with both of them now. I do the same thing with my children as I'd do if I talked to a school full of kids. I put it in simple terms. I tell them it's like playing Russian roulette with a gun. Drugs and alcohol do the same thing. You never know you're an alcoholic or an addict until you are one, and then you can never change that. It stays forever. Like when you're dead, you're dead."

He still can't explain why, despite all the public service announcements and all the stories, people do drugs. "If I knew the answer … " He paused. "I had a guy ask me, 'How could you go out and use coke again right after Len Bias died?' My answer to that was, 'How could Len Bias go out and do coke when he saw what happened to me?'

"Addiction is a disease. People have an arrogance that says, 'It won't happen to me.' Denial is the biggest stumbling block, whether it's food, sex, gambling, drugs. It's the denial that you have the problem. If I wanted to continue using, I could justify it. I could find someone a lot worse off than me and say, 'Well, I'm not as bad as him.' "

The smoke from the cigarette in Steve Howe's right hand curled upward. The steam seeped from the fresh, hot cup of coffee in front of him. He smiled impishly over the breakfast table at the Radisson Bay Harbor Inn, where the Yankees were staying for last weekend's games in Clearwater and Sarasota.

"Nicotine definitely is a drug," Howe acknowledged. "So's caffeine. So's coffee. Tea. You're eating chemicals. Some of it is mood-altering sugar. People eat it every day. If people say Steve Howe's going to have a problem because smoking's a drug, I'll tell them, 'You take drugs, too, and my life is just as under control as yours is.'

"I've been smoking since I was 16. It's my choice. I know when I quit the vigorous exercise I do now, I'm going to quit smoking. I'm not ready now."

(March 24, 1991)

~ *Steve Howe pitched for the Yankees for six of his twelve Major League seasons with mixed results until being released in June 1996. He spent the 1997 season with Sioux Falls of the independent Northern League before retiring. Howe was 48 when he died April 28, 2006, after being thrown from his pickup truck when it drifted off a desert highway and rolled over several times in Coachella, Calif., about 150 miles east of Los Angeles. Toxicological results determined there was methamphetamine, an illegal drug, in his bloodstream.* ~

Two

'I will sail alone rather than not sail at all'

By the time dawn broke, Webb Chiles had accepted death, waiting for it to wash over him like the ocean chop that tossed him about. But death would not come.

Sleep would come - but only for an instant. One moment he would be treading water, the next he would doze off. His head would slip beneath the surface and he would inhale a bit of the Atlantic Ocean. He would awake with a sputtering gasp and find himself wincing as a thousand needles of sunlight glanced off the ripples and burned into his eyes.

And then the sun was gone and the blackness enveloped him again.

Off in the distance, he could see the lights of a fishing boat. He swam toward it. A mile away. Then half a mile. Help me, he called, his voice a rasping, hollow croak.

The fishermen weighed anchor and powered away.

Well then, he said to himself, don't help me.

It was about 24 hours now since Resurgam, Webb Chiles' 36-foot Sparkman and Stephens sloop, had suddenly and inexplicably begun taking on water about 1 in the morning on Aug. 15. In a matter of minutes, it had sunk about 12 miles off the coast of Fort Lauderdale.

Chiles could have grabbed one of the life jackets. But having been in survival situations before, he knew one can't swim very effectively in a life jacket. So he ignored them as the flotsam and jetsam of his life swirled around him.

He had become Resurgam's second owner in 1983, had spent the better part of nine years refurbishing and retooling it. It had been brought to a level of perfection. Now it was gone.

All of Chiles' possessions - everything - had gone down with the boat. All that he owned he now wore. A T-shirt. Shorts. And, in a pocket, a billfold with a credit card.

He made sure to take it along, he said, recalling those final few frantic moments aboard Resurgam, so that if his body was ever recovered, the credit card might be the only way to identify it.

Plastic, he thought to himself, is not biodegradable. I am.

Fire down below

Webb Chiles is 51. He has circumnavigated the globe three times and was working on his fourth when Resurgam went down. He has been married five times to four women, for as much as seven years, for as little as six months. His latest marriage is just coming to an end.

He has lived most of the past 25 years on boats - sailing, writing, lecturing, teaching and making boat deliveries. "I have no family," he said. He is an only child and is still figuratively running away from home.

Home was Kirkwood, Mo., a middle-class suburb of St. Louis. His father died when he was a little boy. His mother was a housewife, his stepfather a steel mill executive.

"Mark Twain, a fellow Missourian, once said all adventure begins with books and all adventurers begin by running away from home," Chiles said. "Mine began with books. I didn't like the Midwest. Still don't. I've been around the world a good many times and the Midwest is one of the dullest places on the planet. I always wanted to get out."

He read sailing and yachting magazines and pored over each issue of National Geographic. He first saw the ocean, the Atlantic, from St. Augustine when his grandparents were looking for a place to retire. They eventually settled in San Diego and Chiles spent his summers as a teen-ager in the company of the Pacific.

Then, when he was 16, came Fire Down Below.

"There was a scene in the movie," Chiles recalled, "where Rita Hayworth steps up to the bow of a boat and dives off and swims ashore to some Caribbean island and the water is beautiful and the beach is white and pristine and the palm trees . . .

"And I remember walking home on a snowy, bleak and, worst of all, landlocked Midwestern winter night and dreaming that one day I would go with a woman like that on a boat like that to an island like that. And I forgot that dream for 30 years.

"And I sailed around the world twice before ever going to the Caribbean. And one day when Jill and I were anchored off of Virgin Gorda in the British Virgin Islands, Jill walked up to the bow of the boat and stood poised for a moment before she dove in the water and swam ashore and suddenly it came to me that I had done it. I had gone with a woman like that on a boat like that to an island like that."

'Not yet'

His eyes and mouth, splashed thousands of times by the Atlantic, had long ago become raw wounds.

"For the first nine hours I was Socrates, completely calm and accepting," Chiles said. "I was 50, a good swimmer in very good shape,

11

but didn't think I could make it to shore. There was no panic, no fear, because I expected to die. Maybe it was an offshoot of being a philosophy major. Socrates' attitude toward death after he took the hemlock was, "'Why should I be afraid of death? When I am, death is not, and when death is, I am not.' "

He treaded water and waited. "I thought dying would be relatively quick and easy. In fact, it was very long and never happened. I became bored waiting for it to happen and I became Dylan Thomas: 'Do not go gentle into that good night.' I struggled, struggled hard. But I was in control. I started trying to make it to shore."

He had been carried northeast by the current. The Florida coastline had fallen away. He was in the north-south shipping channel, out of sight of land.

If there were any ships nearby, his chances of seeing them or being seen were drowned in a driving rainstorm.

The rain abated. An occasional fishing boat would appear out of the mist, then vanish back into it, its crewmen oblivious to Chiles' shouts. Freighters were visible - but too far away. Had they been closer, Chiles' cry for help would have been drowned out by the thrum of their engines.

And the darkness came again. And somewhere in the warmth of the Gulf Stream, Saturday became Sunday.

And on and on he swam - 20 of one stroke, 20 of another, 20 of yet another, then treading water, then just floating, trying to wash away the exhaustion.

As he lay motionless in the water, little fish would nibble at his hands and feet. He would shake them away and say, both to them and himself, not yet.

Gales and cyclones

Webb Chiles earned his bachelor of arts degree from the University of Dubuque, took some graduate courses in philosophy at the University of California at Berkeley, bought his first boat - a cramped 26-footer - and he and the woman with whom he was living at the time moved aboard.

He has lived almost exclusively on the water ever since.

He got bored with school and became, as he put it, a petty bureaucrat, working for about 10 years for the California Department of Vocational Rehabilitation. Just a way to pay for bigger boats, he said. He planned some day to sail around Cape Horn, the southernmost tip of South America.

On a Friday afternoon in 1974 he withdrew his money from the state retirement fund and closed his bank account. On Saturday morning, he set sail. "I think I knew when I left," he said, "that I would never be able to return to a normal life."

He has sailed around the world three times, once by himself in a Drascombe Lugger, an 18-foot open boat that looks like a rowing dory with a small mast - the smallest boat ever to make the voyage.

He has ridden out gales and cyclones, and once survived a capsizing by climbing into an inflatable life raft and floating for two weeks between Fiji and the New Hebrides. He has spent months at sea without hearing the sound of a human voice - not even his own.

An uninsurable life

He had been in the Atlantic for nearly 30 hours. He was starting to hallucinate. But he wasn't so far gone that he didn't know he was hallucinating.

The moon was full and the bottom of one bright cloud was transformed into a lace doily. He knew it wasn't real, but the vision persisted.

Then off to the side Chiles thought he saw a large sailboat at anchor. No sails. No running lights. He wasn't sure if it was there or not - but he had to swim somewhere, so why not toward an apparition?

As he got closer, he saw an anchor light. It was a sailboat. It was at anchor, yet it seemed to be powering away from him. He cried out. Once. Twice. A voice called back.

Two young men, commercial fisherman a few miles off the Sebastian Inlet, had been asleep. One of them thought he heard a voice in a dream. Then it woke him, he clambered up on deck and shouted into the darkness.

"Don't go away!" Chiles wailed.

They weren't going anywhere. Chiles was being carried past them by the Gulf Stream. The fishermen illuminated a searchlight, followed Chiles' voice until they found him, urged him to the boat and pulled him aboard.

"My first thought wasn't, 'I'm going to live,' " Chiles recalled. "It was, 'I'm going to get a drink of water.' "

Chiles was nauseous, sore, exhausted and sunburned. But he needed no medical attention. A few weeks later he was back on a borrowed boat, back at sea.

Resurgam had flares and life jackets aboard, but only because the Coast Guard required them. It didn't have the recommended emergency radio equipment. "I don't think they're useful," Chiles said. "In most of the world, nobody's going to get to you before you're dead anyway. …

"When you're a solo sailor, you have no right to expect society to come look for you. You should be responsible for yourself. All these safety devices, these are shore-committee kinds of things, the effluvium of a litigious society.

"I have lived a life, by choice, at risk," he said, "an uninsured and uninsurable life. By and large, no one will write insurance for solo sailing."

'A sailor is an artist'

People ask him if he has a death wish. His answer is that after 25 years of adventure, he is still here. "I'm neither lucky nor unlucky. People who are professionals, and I am one, don't take unnecessary risks. I don't claim to be brave. People are usually afraid of the unfamiliar, and these things aren't unfamiliar to me."

But why live this life?

The philosophy major in Webb Chiles emerges with a rush.

"A sailor is an artist whose medium is the wind," he says at one moment.

And later. "Live passionately, even if it kills you, because something's going to kill you anyway."

And still later: "I enjoy solitude, settling into the rhythms of the sea, the way of life, carrying everything with me in a limited space. I like music. I like books. And I still spend part of each day just looking at the waves. For me, that's home.

"I have words and I have passion and women know that and I think it attracts them. To some extent, perhaps it overwhelms them. While they like the romance and passion, they eventually need security, too. I don't speak badly of any of them."

If - when - Webb Chiles weighs anchor and sets sail again, he expects he will not do it solo. "I don't think I have anything more to learn from solitude, but I will sail alone rather than not sail at all," he said. "It was important at one time for me to sail around the world alone, to set world records. Which I did. Once I knew I could do that, that wasn't important anymore.

"My choice is to find another woman to spend my life with. I have been in love in some very good places. The South Pacific is my favorite part of the world. My plan was to complete the fourth circumnavigation and then to remain there, sailing from Tahiti to Australia with an occasional jaunt to Bali.

"I expected to end this voyage needing only money. Now I need money, a woman and a boat. Still, it wasn't a bad plan."

(January 15, 1993)

~ Webb Chiles was the first American to sail solo around Cape Horn, the southernmost point of South America. He has circumnavigated the globe five times, holds several world records, and has written numerous books on sailing. ~

Three

Making a name for himself

There still are demons. Maybe that's why Danny Hurley doesn't want to shoot too high.

"I just want to be good, not great," he says. "If I'm great, people are going to want me to be great all the time. I don't want to set goals for myself and then come up short. I come up short, I'll start to feel bad about myself again, view myself as a failure."

Danny Hurley is the basketball player who could never be Bobby Hurley. He went to Seton Hall, not Duke. He was coached by the rigid P. J. Carlesimo, not the more flexible Mike Krzyzewski. He is a shooting guard, not a playmaker.

Not that he ever wanted to be another Bobby. But everyone else, it sometimes seemed, expected him to be. So Danny Hurley allowed a sibling rivalry that was never really there to take control of his psyche and rub it so raw that he quit the game he loved most.

"He gets paralysis by analysis," says his father, Bob, a probation officer and, for 21 years, a highly successful coach at St. Anthony, a small Catholic school in Jersey City, N.J.

"Danny keeps planning, plotting. He just won't relax and let things happen."

"Danny is his own worst enemy and always has been," adds his mother, Christine, a preschool teacher. "It has nothing to do with Bobby, has nothing to do with Bob. We never expected Bobby to do what he's doing now (playing in the NBA). We never said to them, 'We want you to play ball, we want you to go to Duke, to Seton Hall, to become a pro.' But Danny will overanalyze everything he does. We try to, what, underanalyze?"

Growing up as the kid brother of a basketball superstar - and the son of a neighborhood basketball genius - never is easy. Like it or not, there is a reputation to uphold. Being born a Hurley in Jersey City, you might as well be born a Sinatra in Hoboken.

A little more than a year ago, Danny Hurley's world imploded, first in the shambles of the worst game of his career and then, two weeks later, a coast away where Bobby lay broken and bleeding in the wreckage of an auto accident.

Bobby's body has healed. He is back in the NBA. Danny's psyche has healed, too. He is, he says, enjoying basketball again. Playing it rather well, too. He carries a 14.2-point scoring average, second on the team, and 4.9 assist average into Seton Hall's Big East Conference game tonight in Miami.

"I look at each game as an opportunity to have fun. And to prove some people wrong. That's what motivates me now - all those people who gave up on me."

Danny Hurley is 22 years old, 18 months younger than Bobby. In each of the six seasons one or both played for St. Anthony, the school was state champion. In Bobby's senior year, he was Gatorade Player of the Year and St. Anthony was 32-0 and USA Today national champion. In Danny's senior year, he was Gatorade Player of the Year and St. Anthony was 32-1 and No. 2 nationally.

For two years they played side-by-side in the backcourt. Long before and long after, they played as teammates - in playgrounds and, a couple of years ago in front of hundreds of people in summer-league games on the Jersey shore.

"The only people who made comparisons, and they still do, are sports writers and TV people and fans," Christine Hurley said. "But if there was a problem with either one thinking the other one was better, they couldn't have played together."

Maybe it wasn't a problem, Danny said, "but the burden of being a Hurley was always there. Growing up, maybe I was envious, jealous at times."

Bobby was a two-time All-American, a member of Duke's two-time national champions and MVP of the 1992 Final Four as a junior. He averaged 13.2 points in 1991-92 and 17 the next season.

Danny Hurley averaged 2.8 points for Seton Hall in 1991-92 and 6.1 the next season.

'A very bad choice'

Danny Hurley could have gone to Duke or any of the dozens of schools that recruited him. He wanted to stay home. "Bobby was eight hours away by car; when you have the income my wife and I have it's by car. It's certainly not flying back and forth," the elder Hurley said. "Danny wanted to be closer, wanted to be able to get a good meal." Hurley chose the Hall.

It was, Bob said, "a very bad choice. He's a lefty and he spent two years of his college career dribbling with the other hand down the other side of the court. It's like turning a real good right-handed hitter around just to get him a step closer to first. Bobby'd played on great teams and had great freedom. Danny was playing in a structured system that was strangling him, and he had (Carlesimo) screaming at him all the time."

Bob and Christine Hurley would ask their younger son if he was sure he wanted to stay at Seton Hall, if he wouldn't rather transfer and enjoy himself more.

Danny was stubborn. He would be successful, no matter the price.

"Bobby'd had to live up to our father. That was tough enough," Danny said. "I thought I had to live up to both of them. That's tougher. By the time I was a junior, I'd decided it was my turn to be a great player, to put up the big numbers."

'I really needed that'

The first game last season, Hurley hit 2 of 11 shots in a 59-46 win over St. Peter's at the Meadowlands, Seton Hall's home court. He was booed vociferously, as he had been much of the previous season.

"After a while," he said, "I'd look forward to playing road games. I didn't want to have to play at home."

If Danny had gone to, say, an ACC school like Duke, his father said, he would have played in a smaller arena on campus, the court surrounded by students. "Every arena in the Big East is huge, off campus. You don't get as many students. It's more like corporate America involved in college basketball, a lot of bettors.

"At the Meadowlands, anyone who buys a Seton Hall season ticket goes into the lottery or the NCAA (regional tournament at the arena). So you don't get a true home court. They're not true fans. A lot of them are just there for a shot at the NCAAs."

Game 2. Dec. 4, 1993. It was being called Hurley Day at the Garden. Bobby, a Sacramento rookie, would play the New York Knicks that afternoon; Danny Hurley and the Pirates would play St. John's in the evening. Everyone - parents, friends and a lot of Jersey City - would be there.

"Hurley Day," Danny repeated with a wry little laugh. "I really needed that."

Danny watched the NBA game from the team's hotel room. Bobby had a mediocre game - 3-for-6, six points - in the Kings' 123-101 loss. "I wanted to be there," Danny said, "but Coach Carlesimo wouldn't let me out.

"The whole day I felt this enormous pressure building. I'd been struggling. I needed a big game."

Danny took six shots, three from three-point range. He missed all six. He had 2 assists, 4 rebounds and 1 point when Carlesimo benched him. St. John's won 72-64.

"I tried to do too much. I was terrible," Danny said. "I didn't leave my room for four or five days after that game. I couldn't eat, couldn't look at anyone; I thought they were looking at me and thinking, 'failure.' I think I was close to having a nervous breakdown."

Danny had never sat down with his father and mother and hashed out his problems. "I didn't want to go to my parents. I thought they'd be disappointed in me." Now he told them, and Bobby, that he couldn't take it anymore. A week after the Madison Square Garden debacle, Danny Hurley quit.

The only disappointment, his father said, was that Danny hadn't come to him before. "Funny thing," Bob Hurley said. "Every kid I've ever coached who's had a problem in college has called me. But not Danny. It was eating away at him for the longest time, but he wanted to work it out himself."

'I felt so worthless'

On Dec. 11, 1993, Carlesimo said Danny Hurley had taken a leave of absence for undisclosed personal reasons. On Dec. 12, after the Kings had lost to the visiting Los Angeles Clippers, Bobby Hurley's Toyota 4Runner was broadsided by a station wagon while making a left turn about a mile from Arco Arena.

Hurley, not wearing his seat belt, was thrown about 80 feet and down an embankment into a water-filled ditch. He had five broken ribs, collapsed lungs, a severed windpipe, a fractured shoulder blade and other injuries.

The Hurley family flew to California.

"I kept wondering why it wasn't me in that hospital bed," Danny said. "I was crying, wishing it was me instead of him. I mean, it just seemed he had so much to live for, had so much going for him, and I was just this guy who couldn't even finish his college career without quitting. I felt so worthless."

Winter slid by. Danny helped Bobby with his running, his weight training, his exercises, rebuilding his body. Bobby told Danny he wasn't a failure, that he had too much talent not to do well, rebuilding his spirit.

Danny rejoined his team in late January, practicing but not playing. Bobby resumed basketball practice in April and, within two months, was playing in summer leagues with Danny.

In June, Carlesimo left Seton Hall for the NBA's Portland Trail Blazers. Holy Cross coach George Blaney succeeded him.

Suddenly Seton Hall was a running, free-wheeling team - Hurley's game. "It's fun," he said, "almost as much fun as high school."

Danny Hurley says he could not have imagined a year ago having this good of a season. "It seems like so long ago that all that stuff happened." But he also says he must remain on guard.

"Bobby was able to put his accident behind him," Danny says. "Physically, he's whole again. Mentally, every day I have to fight to stay positive. It's still a struggle. If I have a bad game, and I've had a few this season, it bothers me for a few minutes, then I put it behind me. I know now that it has nothing to do with the kind of person I am.

"And if I do get upset, it's just because I had a bad game," Danny Hurley added, "not because I'm not Bobby Hurley."

(February 22, 1995)

~ *Unlike his brother Bobby, who played five seasons in the NBA, Danny Hurley went directly from Seton Hall into coaching. He built St. Benedict's Prep in New Jersey into a national high school power, coached Wagner College for two seasons, then took over at Rhode Island University before the 2011-2012 season.* ~

Four

For dying children, a long shot

MARCO ISLAND - The football metaphors come easily to Ara Parseghian. He talks about being in the fourth quarter with the clock running. He mentions how his team is desperate to get the winning score. He says he knows there's no overtime.

They are understandable, considering his 24 years as a head coach and three national championships at Notre Dame. But in a world in which football is often treated as a matter of life and death and players are regarded as heroes, Parseghian also understands how the hyperbole pales beside the reality.

Three of his grandchildren are dying.

The killer is Niemann-Pick Type C. It is a genetic disease. There is no way to test carriers of the disease. There is no way to know of its presence until symptoms appear. Then it is too late. Even before symptoms appear, it is too late. There is no cure.

If both parents are carriers of the defective gene ... and that is the only way Niemann-Pick can be passed along ... statistics suggest there is only a 1-in-4 chance that any of their children will inherit the disease.

Michael Parseghian is the youngest of Ara and Katie's three children. Michael and Cindy and their four children live in Tucson, Ariz.

Ara, 11, is the oldest. He is fine. The others are Michael, 8, Marcia, 6, and Christa, 4. They have Niemann-Pick Type C. Three of four. The statistics that have brutally cheated the Parseghian family suggest that young Michael, Marcia and Christa will die within a decade.

Ara Parseghian is 71. He and Katie split their year between South Bend and a seventh-floor penthouse on Marco Island overlooking a picture-postcard expanse of white sand and, beyond, the Gulf of Mexico. They shouldn't have a care in the world.

Instead, much of Ara Parseghian's world is a swirl of checks and pledges and speaking engagements and conferences … with Katie immersed in correspondence and paperwork … in the desperate pursuit to cure an orphan disease.

"My grandchildren, they're here now,'" he says. "The rules say they can last into their early teens. Give me some time. The score is tied. I can't afford a tie. Give me another quarter. I can win this game."

The Ara Parseghian Medical Research Foundation has, in its first six months, raised $1-million. Cindy is the retired president of a cable TV company and, like her husband, a summa cum laude graduate of Notre Dame. "She takes care of the kids and runs the blood and guts of the foundation," says Michael, an orthopedic surgeon.

"People tell me I'm heroic," Cindy Parseghian says. "You know, you would do this, too, and it's not heroic. It's very selfish. If we do nothing we know the outcome, and that's unacceptable. I know other children will benefit, but I'm doing this in the hope I can save my children."

Looking for a cosmic explanation

Orphan disease. Ironic phrase, that. It is the children who die, the parents who survive.

But in the bottom-line world we live in, it means Niemann-Pick Type C is not catastrophic enough to command serious attention from the big drug companies, the big foundations, the government. It is not AIDs or cancer or muscular dystrophy.

There are perhaps 500 children in the United States diagnosed with Niemann-Pick Type C, perhaps several thousand in this country and the rest of the world who have gone undiagnosed. The disease doesn't affect enough people, therefore, there isn't enough money to be made off of it. There are no Jerry Lewis telethons. There are no poster children. So, like many other orphan diseases, it goes under-funded and under-researched. Or ignored.

Which is part of why Ara Parseghian has mustered all his energy to finding a cure for this very obscure, always fatal disease.

"Maybe there is a pattern to all of this," says Katie Parseghian, looking for a cosmic explanation. "Maybe it has to do with name recognition, bringing attention to it that it has never had before. Maybe if this had been Joe Blow's kids who got it, nobody'd have known what it is. And maybe this terrible thing wouldn't be getting the attention it's getting now. And maybe it would be years more before a cure was found. Maybe it's why these children were chosen."

'He'll grow out of it'

Niemann-Pick is a storage disease. That is, it prevents the body from metabolizing cholesterol, causing it to accumulate within liver, spleen and brain cells, killing them. The resulting damage causes, among other symptoms, slurred speech, loss of balance and motor skills, and seizures. And, five to 10 years after the symptoms appear, death.

Young Michael Parseghian's parents figured three years ago that something was wrong. He just wasn't keeping up with the other children. His handwriting was failing. His motor skills weren't up to par for kindergarten.

"We started taking him to physicians," Cindy Parseghian said. "Our first pediatrician looked at me and laughed and said, 'Oh, he's a little clumsy for his age but if he was my child I wouldn't do anything.' But he was my child, and I felt it just wasn't right."

One pediatrician and neurologist after another kept saying the same thing. Don't worry. He'll grow out of it. Eventually the path took the Parseghians to Columbia University in New York last June. In one five-minute examination, a neuropathologist, noticing young Michael's neurological difficulties and enlarged spleen, suggested Niemann-Pick Type C. Two months of testing confirmed the diagnosis.

Worse, the Parseghians knew their daughters had been born with enlarged spleens. The girls were displaying no neurological problems. Still, they (and Ara, their older brother) were tested. The girls' tests came up positive.

Niemann-Pick is a degenerative disease. There is no treatment for the disease, only for its symptoms. Michael, Marcia and Christa are on special diets and take cholesterol-reducing drugs, which have reduced the cholesterol level in their cardiovascular systems.

"Maybe that slows down the disease," Ara Parseghian said, "and if we can slow it down, maybe that gives us more time to find a cure."

Even if a cure is found, it might do no more than halt the damage. Brain tissue does not repair itself very well.

Marcia is in kindergarten now. Her handwriting is getting worse. She is beginning to experience a slight motor tremor. When she was 4, she was the first one in her ballet class to jump, the first one to tie her shoes. Now her classmates are passing her. Christa, except for a problem with jumping, looks and acts like any other typical 4 year old.

'This is the first step'

In September, the Parseghian family grieved.

"I would sit in the car by myself and break down," Ara said. "I couldn't get past the question: Why? Why these kids?"

Cindy's beliefs were shaken. "I'd always had a really strong faith in God," she said. "This made me think a lot about it, about what kind of God is out there. Maybe he's not all-powerful like we all thought he was."

For her husband, the frustration lay in the fact that he, a physician dedicating his life to healing, could do nothing medically for his children.

"I'm not so idealistic to believe that medicine can do everything," Michael Parseghian said. "But when you sit on the other side of the table, hearing things about your own family that you, as a doctor, usually tell other people, it becomes more of a reality."

After the grieving process had run its course - not that it ever really does - Cindy and Michael decided to do more, to form a foundation to research this strange disease that had suddenly become the focal point of their lives.

They asked Ara for help. He said he would do anything. By November, the foundation had been formed. By December it had been granted tax-free status and Michael Parmacek had come aboard.

He and Michael Parseghian have been friends since medical school. Parmacek is a cardiologist and molecular biologist at the University of Chicago. He jumped into learning about Niemann-Pick, then helped assemble the seven-member scientific advisory board, the geneticists, pathologists and molecular biologists that are the core of the foundation.

"We decided to target our research to specific goals, things that could be achieved in time frames - and things that might have relevance to Mike and his family," Parmacek said.

First, find the gene responsible for Niemann-Pick. Second, create an "assay system" to enable drug companies to test hundreds of thousands of compounds to see if they affect the disease.

"Every gene makes one protein," Parmacek explained. "If we can replace the protein made by the defective gene, we could theoretically cure the disease. There are diseases where that has happened. Gaucher's and Tay-Sachs are the two most common storage diseases (both, like Niemann-Pick, involving the accumulation of fat). Tay-Sachs isn't cured. Gaucher's is."

The Parseghian foundation will fund more than $1-million in research this year. It sounds like a lot of money. In one sense, it is a lot, perhaps 10 times as much as was spent last year. But in terms of what it takes to cure a disease, it is virtually nothing.

"I told Mike we'd have to raise at least $1-million before we could even think of funding laboratories," Parmacek said. "To make any significant progress it'll take more like $10-million.

"This is the first step. It gets us off the ground. I believe we can isolate the gene in two years at the outside, maybe within one. On the other hand, that's the easiest part. We've known the gene for cystic fibrosis for four years. We've made progress, but it's not cured yet."

Is there hope for Michael, Marcia and Christa Parseghian?

"It's a long shot at best," Parmacek said. "We all understand that. But Niemann-Pick can be somewhat unpredictable. The average child, once the disease is diagnosed, lives five to 10 years. But some survive into their 20s. If that's the case here, yes, there's hope. If not …"

Guilt

Ara and Katie's older children, Karan and Kristan also are married. Karan, her husband and two sons live in Akron, Ohio. Kristan, her husband and three daughters live outside of South Bend, Ind. The children, from the low teens to the 20s, are healthy.

This month, the Parseghian children and their spouses and all nine grandchildren converged on Marco Island.

"We're over-run," Katie said. "When there's that many kids, all the activity, all the noise, all the dirty dishes and laundry, getting all the kids glopped with sunscreen so they can go on the beach, you feel like everything's okay."

The Parseghians spoil all their grandchildren equally. They try hard to not give special treatment to Michael, Marcia and Christa. It is 11-year-old Ara who seems to catch Katie's eye in an unguarded moment, when her emotional defenses are down.

"I'm very protective of him," she said. "It's like, Please, God, don't let anything happen to Ara, too.' I'm ready to wrap him in plastic."

In a different way, Cindy and Michael Parseghian, too, worry about their 11-year-old son "as much as the other three, maybe even more," Cindy said. "We worry about the long-term impact on him," fearing that young Ara might suffer the guilt experienced by the survivors of tragedies. And for now, she added, "Ara needs to live as normal a life as possible. We don't want him to get lost in the shuffle."

It is the very normality of life that can add to the frustration. Michael, Marcia and Christa Parseghian are, after all, flesh-and-blood children, not microbes in a petri dish. They do all the stuff that kids do to drive their parents nuts.

"We get angry with them, sure," Cindy said. "We yell at them, and it really is guilt-laden whenever we do it, when we haven't taken that extra moment."

31

Cindy Parseghian is one tough parent, ferociously proud and protective of her children, very matter-of-fact about the disease that is slowly stealing them away from her. Yet the terrible emotional reality of it is never far from her consciousness.

"I have learned more from Michael," she says, a tremor in her voice, "because that child loves life, he loves himself, and every disability he has, he diminishes it and keeps moving. Every night we say prayers around the table and he thanks God for a good day, no matter what happens. "

'Dreams and aspirations'

The girls haven't made the correlation between Michael's increasing disabilities and the emerging erosion of their own motor skills. "They just accept Michael as he is," their mother said. Marcia, though, is astute enough to wonder why she can't draw pictures while the girl next to her can."

There is a long silence.

"I don't take anything for granted with these kids," Cindy Parseghian says. "We've always spent a lot of time together as a family; I don't know that that has changed. But every moment with them is pretty bittersweet. … People ask me, 'How do you get out of bed in the morning? How do you not just pull the covers back over you?' It's . . ."

More silence.

"It's the children. I look at them as living, not as dying. They have dreams and aspirations just like any other child, and they're not always long-term dreams. They're about Michael getting his blue belt in karate or Marcia's ballet recital coming up. I, as a parent - as any parent - want to make those dreams and aspirations come true."

The steel in Cindy Parseghian's voice is returning, if only for a moment.

"That's what keeps us going, that and the incredible support from our family and friends who encourage us, keep us moving, keep us focused, keep us pursuing a cure. … There's a part of me …"

More silence.

" … a part of me that thinks these children won't be here in 10 years. Two or three, yes, they'll be with me. But, yes, it's always back there, that fear, that knowledge. Lots of times I try to bury it, but it's never much below the surface. Is it just bad luck? I don't know. I feel incredibly unlucky. But you live with it."

(May 16, 1995)

Michael Parseghian died March 22, 1997. He was 9.
Christa Parseghian died October 3, 2001. She was 10.
Marcia Parseghian died August 6, 2005. She was 13.

ABOUT THE DISEASE

Niemann-Pick Type C disease is an extremely rare and fatal genetic disease that strikes children and makes them unable to metabolize cholesterol properly. There is no cure. As the disease progresses, cholesterol accumulates in major organs like the liver, spleen and brain, causing damage to the nervous system. Children with the disease often are symptom-free in early childhood, but symptoms worsen over time. Symptoms include slurred speech, loss of balance and muscular control and memory loss. In the later stages, symptoms can be similar to those of Alzheimer's disease. The final phase of Niemann-Pick Type C brings on dementia, seizures and death. Victims usually die by age 20. The cause of death often is a complication such as pneumonia. Niemann-Pick Type C is so rare that experts estimate there are only between 300 to 500 cases in the United States. The odds of acquiring the disease is 1 in 640,000, about the same as being struck by lightning.

Tax-deductible contributions to the Ara Parseghian Medical Research Foundation can be sent to:

4729 E Sunrise Drive, #327

Tucson, Ariz. 85718-4535
Phone: (520) 577-5106
E-Mail: promano@parseghian.org

Five

Like coach, like son

His hair is beginning to thin and what remains is beginning to gray. He is 42 and in his eighth season as coach of the DePaul Blue Demons. But he still hasn't entirely lost that choir-boy look.

And he has always been and still is Joey.

Not Joseph (which is what it says on his birth certificate).

Not Joe.

Joey.

"You know how when you're young you want to look old and when you're old you want to look young?" Joey Meyer muses. "I think I'm beginning to really appreciate being Joey. I think I'll appreciate it more and more as I get older."

And whatever they call him, wherever he coaches, he's still Ray's boy.

"Maybe if he'd been a Smith or a Jones, maybe if he'd been Joe Blow and gone somewhere else, life would've been easier for him," said Ray Meyer, who coached DePaul basketball for 42 years, becoming as much of an institution in downtown Chicago as the campus under the El on West Belden Avenue.

"Hindsight," Joey said, "tells me that taking over for Coach was a lot tougher than I thought it was going to be."

In 1984-85, his first season, Joey's team went 19-10, the first time in eight seasons DePaul hadn't won 20 games. They were invited to the NCAA Tournament and lost to Syracuse in the first round.

The next year, the Blue Demons were 18-13. He heard the boos, the questions, the criticism. Was he too young? Was he in on a pass 'cause he was the old man's kid?

"I began feeling sorry for myself," he said.

The Blue Demons really didn't belong in the NCAA Tournament that year. Still, they beat Virginia in the opening round. Then they shocked Oklahoma. And in the Sweet 16, they nearly upset Duke.

"Being fortunate enough to get into the tournament and go that far, and then coming back with a 28-3 season, I think that helped get me out from Coach's shadow," Joey said. "Now people get on my case because I'm screwing up on my own, not because I'm Coach's kid."

He was always 'Coach'

Coach. That's what everybody calls Ray. That's what Joey calls him. Not dad. Coach.

"I'm not entirely sure where it started," Joey said, "but when I was playing for him, I didn't want to call him dad. I wanted to be just one of the players."

Oh, it started way before that. It started when Ray was at St. Patrick's in Chicago, the year after he and his St. Pat's teammates won the National Catholic High School Championship.

Ray wasn't playing basketball as a senior in 1933. But a priest at St. Agatha's shanghaied Ray into helping coach his girls CYO parish league team. Marge Delaney was on the team. She was 17, too. She called him Coach.

After a month or so, Ray and Marge began keeping company. They continued dating when he went to Notre Dame and for two years afterward. When she died in 1985, they'd been married for 46 years. "She always called me Coach," Ray said, "so the children did, too." The grandchildren ... 16 of them and one great-grandchild ... call him grandpa.

The children. "My wife raised them," Ray said. "I don't take any credit." Five of them are DePaul graduates. Barbara (she attended DePaul for a couple of years before getting married) works in an airline payroll office. Patricia is in the DePaul treasurer's office. Mary Anne and Tommy are schoolteachers. Robert is a lawyer.

Joey, fourth in line, was the quiet one, the shy one.

"I remember this one Easter Sunday," Ray said. "I was taking movies of all the kids. Their mother had dressed them all up for church. Joey, he was about 10, and I was trying to get him coming down the front steps with all the other children and he didn't want his picture taken. He started to turn back and I was calling him and he was crying and his mother was whacking him."

'He didn't want to coach'

Joey was growing up in a house with an old-fashioned father figure. "Coach was never the type to hug, to kiss, to express feelings," Joey said. "He was definitely the authoritarian. Mom could always say, 'Wait till your father gets home.'"

Of course, Ray Meyer wasn't a legend then. "Back in the '50s, DePaul wasn't that big of a deal and he was just another coach," Joey said. "My father didn't really get to be big, so to speak, until the last few years. I think I began to really appreciate him more when he got big because by then I was old enough to understand what Ray Meyer stood for."

And so Joey followed his father's footsteps.

"I didn't want him to coach," Ray said.

"I didn't want to, either," Joey said. "I mean, I never thought about it."

He had graduated from DePaul and was going to go for his master's degree.

And eventually a doctorate in education. He was going to teach.

Northwestern expressed some interest in having Joey as a graduate assistant. Said Ray: "I thought, 'If he's good enough for Northwestern, he's good enough for DePaul.' I approached him and he went along with it. Never did I think he'd stay in coaching."

But after one year as coach of the freshman team, Joey knew it was going to be his life's work. The next year, he coached the junior varsity. When he got his master's degree, he became a full-time assistant.

He became the liaison between Ray and his players, even between Ray and the rest of his staff. "If one of the assistant coaches had a suggestion, they'd ask Joey to ask me," Ray said. "If one of the kids had a problem, they went to Joey. If I jumped on a kid, Joey'd smooth it out.

"It was pretty hard on him sometimes. I felt sorry for him. Players always cut up the head coach, no matter who he is. Joey'd have to listen to people ripping his father."

"Oh, I don't know," Joey offered in rebuttal. "I enjoyed paying my dues. And I think I could do a good job for Coach because I knew what he wanted."

If he did, it wasn't because Coach told him. Maybe Marge. Never Coach.

"Now that my mom has passed away, he has become much more verbal," Joey said. "I used to call my mom the great communicator. You found out what Coach was thinking through her. Even when I was an assistant coach, mom would call me up at home and say, 'Coach is mad at you. Go talk to him.' He wasn't the type to sit down one on one, to initiate a conversation.

"When the family gets together, we tell stories about Coach biting his tongue. That's when he was mad. He chewed on it. When he started doing that, everybody ran. You knew he'd lost it and he was going to get all over your case. Still does it."

'This is Joey's team now'

When the time for a change finally came after the 1983-84 season, "it was much easier for me, knowing Joey was here," Ray said. "It would have been tougher for me to let go if it had been some outsider coming in. With Joey, it was a real easy transition."

They talk to each other more now. Not about basketball … well, not much. "Not X's and O's," Ray said. "Maybe we'll talk about handling players. Mostly we talk about life, about family. I tell Joey how he can't live and die with wins and losses."

Joey Meyer laughs out loud. "When he tells me that, I tell him,'Coach, you couldn't keep from doing it when you were coaching, so don't even think about telling me that. You were one of the worst.'"

These days, Ray Meyer's official title is Special Assistant to the President. What that means is that he speaks to organizations before other DePaul officials hit them up for contributions. He also is color commentator for radio broadcasts of DePaul games.

Coach sits about a dozen feet away from Joey, biting his tongue.

"Many times," Ray said, "I've been tempted to say, 'That's wrong,' or 'That's not how I did it.' But this is Joey's team now. I think he's pretty much moved out of my shadow.

"Y'know, I remember a conversation with Judd Heathcote," he said of the Michigan State coach. "He said he was walking down a hall with one of his players and he mentioned Johnny Wooden and the kid said,'Who's Johnny Wooden?'

"No matter who you are, you eventually fade away. No question about it," Ray Meyer said.

"I'm fading. Joey's growing."

(February 19, 1992)

~ *Joey Meyer was fired by DePaul in 1997. He coached professionally starting in 2000-2001 with the minor-league Chicago Skyliners and later with several NBA Developmental League teams. Ray Meyer died March 17, 2006. He was 92.* ~

Six

On the other side of the nadir point

TAMPA, Fla. - Adam Raskin slipped into the side door of the gymnasium at Tampa Preparatory School. He planned to quietly drop off his uniform before seeking out Susanna Grady, head of the school, and some of his students and fellow teachers.

This was Raskin's first year as a baseball coach and math and physics teacher at Tampa Prep. He didn't know about the tradition on the last day of school – the full assembly to honor the senior class. Every student and teacher was present.

One student noticed Raskin, came down from the bleachers and hugged him. Then another and another, until it was a procession. Mrs. Grady, introducing the seniors, heard the commotion, looked over, then told the assembly, "I have to stop. Mr. Raskin is here."

The applause, the cheers, the hugs and tears of the students and faculty went on and on. It was as if the family was whole again, as if everything was okay, Mrs. Grady was thinking.

Adam Raskin, 27 but with the face of a teenager, stood uncertainly, his shirt and slacks hanging loosely on his frame, exaggerating the weight loss, his Tampa Prep baseball cap hiding the aftermath of the chemotherapy.

Everyone has dreams. Adam Raskin is no different. He grew up in Pittsfield, Mass., dreaming of the day the Boston Red Sox would be World Series champions, of the day he would play big-league baseball.

Dreams don't always come true. Others come along to take their place.

Raskin was a pretty good pitcher. Scouts told him he had a major-league arm - but, at 5 feet 11 and 145 pounds, not the legs, the body to bring the ball at 85 mph.

By his senior year in high school, he knew Division III college baseball was as good as he would be. He would go to Tufts, he decided, and pitch for the small-college team.

A month before school began, his academic scholarship to the University of Massachusetts was approved. A full ride, plus $100 a month in expenses."My dad said, 'You're going to UMass.'"

Raskin made the junior varsity, pitched on opening day and "threw a curveball low-outside to the No. 4 batter. He hit it about 430 feet to right. It was like, 'Welcome to the big time.'" By midseason he knew he should focus on academics.

On Oct. 25, 1986, in his UMass dorm, Raskin and his classmates watched Game 6 of the World Series. The Red Sox, leading the Mets 5-3, were one out away from winning their first World Series since 1918.

Raskin held a bottle of champagne in front of the TV set, the wire already off, his thumb keeping the cork in the bottle. What followed was three singles, a wild pitch and a ground ball that rolled through first baseman Bill Buckner's legs.

Boston lost 6-5. Raskin retied the wire around the cork. "I was physically ill. I knew Game 7 was a *fait accompli*."

Two nights later, the Red Sox lost the World Series.

Raskin was graduated cum laude, a double-major in math and economics. He earned his master's degree from Harvard, and met Myriam Tutoy, who was in hotel restaurant management, then began teaching at Eaglebrook, a prep school about 70 miles from Boston.

Fifteen months ago, after a year-and--half long-distance relationship, Adam and Myriam married. They could live in a dorm at Eaglebrook or he could look for work in Boston.

Even educators with doctorates were out of work in Boston. But Tampa Prep happened to have an opening for a math/physics teacher and was looking for a baseball coach.

The headaches began last December, two months after he had started teaching and coaching at Tampa Prep. None of the doctors could find a cause. Stress, they suggested. Or fatigue.

The headaches got worse. In March, Raskin underwent a CAT scan. It turned up a sinus infection. That's it, the doctors told him, a sinus infection can cause headaches. He was admitted to Centurion Hospital of Carrollwood to undergo surgery.

The blood test, a normal pre-op procedure, was abnormal. A bone-marrow test - drilling into the hip for a biopsy - was conducted.

Just to rule out worst-case scenarios, the doctors said.

Two days later, Raskin's parents arrived in tears at his room. "I knew that wasn't a good sign," he said. That's when the doctor told him it was leukemia. Raskin was transferred to the H. Lee Moffitt Cancer Center in Tampa for chemotherapy.

"Seven days of chemo followed by a seven-day break," Raskin said, "and then the same thing all over again. You have to have the break. It takes a while to recover. The blood count goes down to nothing. It wipes out your bone marrow, but that's the objective. Then the bone marrow can regenerate, hopefully without the leukemia."

The residual effects of chemotherapy can be devastating. The liver and kidneys shut down. Saliva tastes like metal. Headaches and nausea are constant and intense, "like the worst hangover you've ever had, and it won't go away," Raskin said.

In the midst of that, Raskin was given a drug to counteract the nausea. He experienced a neurological reaction. "I was so on edge, so desperate, like, 'This is too much pain. I'm going to die.' Maybe I wanted to die. Maybe I wanted out from all the suffering."

It is called the "nadir point," not only because the blood count is so low and organs are failing, but because the patient has hit rock-bottom emotionally.

"You draw on it," Raskin said. "They're talking about me having bone-marrow transplants. It's not like a kidney operation, where they do it and that's that. You're in rough shape for two, three months. But I know I've been through the nadir point and have made it, so I know I can do it again."

He sat on the veranda at the rear of his Cove Cay condominium, looking at the water below and the nimbostratus clouds in the distance. Myriam was asleep. Rebecca, his sister, was fixing breakfast for Raskin and a guest.

"They say it's therapeutic to look at water, that it calms your nerves," he said. "The pelicans fish in this little estuary. When the mullet run, they're everywhere, hovering and diving."

He paused for a moment.

"You can't stop living. Statistics show that people who stop being positive have less of a chance of survival. Like I tell the kids on the team, 'You walk to the plate and tell yourself you're going to hit the hell out of the ball, you've got a better chance of success than if you go up there hoping you won't strike out.'"

Northside Christian routinely crushes Tampa Prep in baseball. Most teams do. But this year, Prep beat Northside 8-7. "When I think about how serious leukemia is, about what the chance of recovery is, it's like that game. I'd written it off, but the kids came back. That makes me think you can come back from anything."

He is home for three weeks. He will be going back to Moffitt soon for more treatments. He doesn't look far beyond that. He says leukemia has made him live for the moment, to appreciate family, visitors, phone calls, the pelicans diving outside his window.

"I don't look more than a few days down the road now. It doesn't make a hell of a lot of sense. It seems like the last five or six years rushed by ... 'Got to get through college, through grad school, get a job, get furniture.' Things happen for a reason. I've gotten the message that I need to slow down.

"This isn't the Lou Gehrig Story here. I mean, I feel ripped off. I'm too young for this. But it's also made me thankful for what I've had."

Raskin's life is an amalgam of hopes and fears. Lots of fears.

He wants a son. "I love my dad. He was a great role model. But he wasn't an athlete. He didn't have the love of sports I have. I want to have a son and expose him to these things. He may end up a concert violinist and have no love of baseball, but that's okay. I want to have a son and be a father to him in a way that my father wasn't to me."

He may not get the chance to father a child. With the chemotherapy he has had and will need, sterility is a serious possibility. He also thinks about having a son and not being around to see him grow up.

He said his doctors have hinted that these few weeks at home may be his last few weeks at home. He will have to undergo more of the same chemotherapy and probably a bone-marrow transplant. Some people don't make it through the kind of treatment he'll experience.

"Maybe this is some sort of reward," he said. "Some people don't go home for three weeks. I'm home.

"You try not to get your hopes up." Raskin laughed, reflecting on the curse Boston's baseball fans have endured for 74 years. "Like you learn not to get your hopes up about the Red Sox," he said. "It doesn't make sense. History tells you that. But you do, of course. Every year.

"You hear a piece of good news, or you start to feel good, and you get your hopes up. The Sox, they win three in a row and we start talking about a pennant drive. It's natural. With the Sox, of course, they pull at your heart every year and they end up ripping it out. Even though the Sox haven't won in so long, you know it's possible. The odds may be against them based on the past. The same way the odds may be against me."

He has read a lot about leukemia, has sought out different physicians' opinions. "If I'd had this disease 10, 15 years ago, I'd be dead right now. Advances in science have given me a fighting chance. But not a 98 percent chance. It's hard to put numbers to anything.

"They say 20 percent of all patients with my type of leukemia have a prolonged remission. They rarely say 'cure.' But what does 20 percent mean - 20 percent of men between 20 and 30? No, it means infants, 85-year-olds. In many ways, it's probably a coin toss.

"Look, even if they said every person ever diagnosed with this type of illness has died, that doesn't mean the next one's going to die. You can't say the Sox are never going to win a World Series. Some day they're going to win it all. That possibility exists."

He thought for an instant.

"It's probably a stronger possibility that I'm going to come through this thing fine."

Raskin gave a whimsical giggle, propped his feet on the table in front of him and took a bite of his bagel.

"The possibility of survival, of victory, always exists. I don't care if Tampa Prep's going up against the Red Sox. They have a chance. Maybe it's a bit of a stretch, but if there's a metaphor for life, it's there."

(June 5, 1992)

Adam Raskin died January 5, 1994. On October 27, 2004, the Red Sox won their first World Series in 86 years.

Seven

They're ambassadors starting from obscurity

ATLANTA - Roberto Bruni approached with trepidation, if not desperation.

He reached out to shake hands, simultaneously grasping his prey's right elbow so as to prevent retreat.

"You are a journalist?"

There was no need to ask. The bright yellow rectangle with the large black E on my credential was specific enough - and the credential listed name, affiliation and occupation.

Journalist.

"You are here for the West Africans?"

Well, no. An appointment to speak to several athletcs at the Olympic Village had been set up. They had not yet arrived at the media center.

"You will speak to the West Africans?"

Bruni was, in his dignified yet insistent way, pleading.

Behind him was a conference room capable of seating at least 200. At the head table, six microphones stood at mute attention. Behind them, a splash of color, several national flags.

Bruni proffered a business card with the Atlanta 1996 symbol. It identified him as Coordinator, National Olympic Committee Relations.

More accurately, he was in marketing, a promotions director, a public-relations man. His clients this day were the West Africans, five nations, three of them - Cape Verde, Guinea-Bissau, and Sao Tome and Principe - making their Olympic debut.

Bruni had secured the room for three hours. Several days earlier he had sent e-mails to hundreds of print and broadcast journalists from North America and every other continent. He had distributed faxes to hundreds more. Come and meet some of the newest nations in the Olympics, he had said. Meet their athletes, the chefs de mission, heading their delegations.

The athletes and officials stood or sat in small knots, chatting.

No journalists had shown up.

None.

"Please speak to the West Africans," Bruni said.

A deal was cut. After the scheduled interview, if any West Africans remained, I would speak to the West Africans.

Fifty minutes later, they were all there. Still, no other journalists.

Sao Tome and Principe sent two women and two men to the Olympics. Cape Verde sent one woman and three men. Guinea-Bissau sent one man. Period. And the International Olympic Committee paid their way.

"If the IOC does not bring us here free, we do not come," Francisco da Costa, an economist and chef de mission for Guinea-Bissau said, Bruni translating from da Costa's native Portuguese as he did for all the West Africans. "But we do not come here to win medals. We know we do not do that. We are here to meet people we otherwise do not meet. We are members of the international community. We cannot be excluded."

These are the other Olympic nations. And maybe they are the ones that most accurately reflect what Baron Pierre de Coubertin had in mind a century ago when he created these once-purely-amateur Games, that "the most important thing in life is not the triumph but the struggle."

Life in these West African nations is nothing but struggle. They have no billion-dollar Nike campaigns designed to put a gold medal around Michael Johnson's neck. They have no Coca-Colas, Nations-Banks or IBMs to bankroll the building of stadiums and training sites.

They could not afford uniforms for the Olympics. Reebok donated them. They do not have computers to provide statistics. They have no equipment on which to train. "Everything the developed nations take for granted is a struggle," Manuel Jesus Rodrigues, chef de mission of Sao Tome and Principe, said.

"We will not win any medals. We have no hope of that. But we have our pride," he said, pointing at his lapel. "We have our own Olympic pin. With this, we are equal. We make sure they are at every program. We want to be part of the world."

They produce little of anything of value to the rest of the world. They produce barely enough for themselves, if that much. The gross national product of these nations, each of which gained independence from Portugal in the 1970s, is not too much more than Shaquille O'Neal's salary. The average salary is $10 a month.

Sao Tome and Principe hurdler Osvaldo Cassandra Barbosa displayed his Nikes, "I bought these here," he said. "Back home I have . . ." he and Bruni chattered back and forth for a moment, ". . . cloth ones.

"It will be very difficult going home. I have seen what there is (beyond his region's borders) and I will be going away from it. And these," Barbosa pointed to his Nikes, "they will create jealousy."

When you can find Nikes there, they cost about the same as they do here. Imagine spending more than half your annual salary on a pair of sneakers. How badly do you want to be like Mike?

"I train just as hard as Michael Jordan to be an athlete," said Sao Tome and Principe sprinter Pericles Dos Ramos Jesus. "There is frustration that he probably makes more than my country."

His coach, Gervasio Martins de Pina, put a hand on his runner's knee as if to soothe him.

"These are the real athletes," said Jose Manuel vas Fernandes, president of Guinea-Bissau's national Olympic committee. "The real athletes go to compete for themselves, to win medals for their country. To make money from these Games, it cannot happen for us. They do not train under the same conditions. They do not have the time to prepare like the Americans. Their job is to run. It is how they make money."

Antonio Dos Santos Aguiar, president of Sao Tome and Principe's national Olympic Committee, smiled. "An athlete who wins a medal for us," he said, "is a national hero. There is no money, of course. But there is the face on a stamp."

Dos Ramos, 22, said he has seen things here that stretch credulity. Twenty-five dollars to park a car near a venue. People tossing around $100 bills for tickets to events.

"When I was young and I saw America on the television, I thought it was all just a movie, that it could not be true. When I got here, I discovered it was real. I came to realize that America and other countries have what I thought was just make-believe."

Chances are you have never heard of Cape Verde, of Guinea-Bissau, of Sao Tome and Principe. You are not alone, and they know it. And they understand.

"It is a question of culture, of knowledge of geography," vas Fernandes said. "The small fish has to know where the big fish is so as not to be eaten. America does not need to know where Guinea-Bissau is, but we need to know where America is."

And so Cape Verde, Guinea-Bissau and Sao Tome and Principe treat the Olympics not as a sporting event but as a trade show. You have never heard of us, they say to the United States, to Japan, to Nike, to Sony, to the wealth of the world, or if you have, you know little or nothing about us. But we want to be one of you. So come build a factory in our country. Trade with us. Help us to be like you.

The interview ended. No other journalist had shown up.

Roberto Bruni grasped my hand and arm again, thanking me for speaking to the West Africans. Somebody had listened.

As he turned to go, he added, "You will help tell the world?"

(August 3, 1996)

◇ After five Summer Olympics, through the 2012 London Games, neither Cape Verde, Guinea-Bissau nor Sao Tome and Principe has won any medals. ◇

Eight

At Georgetown, everything's done ... Thompson's way

John Thompson Jr. was speaking about the youngster who was doing poorly in class, whose father could not read or write, whose mother was concerned about her son's potential. Eventually the youngster was kicked out of Catholic elementary school. The teachers told his mother he was retarded.

She brought him to a professional educator, a doctor who invited the youngster into his office and asked him to identify objects around the room.

"Radio," the boy said. "Telephone."

Then the boy, overly shy, froze and fell silent.

"You shouldn't be embarrassed," the educator told the woman, "because it's not your fault. But this boy isn't educable."

The boy earned his bachelor's degree in economics and his master's degree in guidance and counseling.

"This little boy," Thompson, said, "is talking to you."

He is far more than the coach of the Georgetown basketball team playing in the Holiday Invitational Wednesday and Thursday at the

Sun Dome in Tampa. He is a complex man, an amalgam of emotions, a man who elicits a full range of emotions from those whose lives he touches.

He is driven to win, but even more to excel. He will needle, threaten or bench his star players if they don't expend every ounce of energy. He will suspend his star players if they fail to produce grades in excess of minimum standards - the National Collegiate Athletic Association's, Georgetown's, and his own.

Some critics say he is more than driven. They say he is an ogre.

He shelters his players as much as he drives them. He protects them in abbreviated locker-room interviews - sometimes timed to the second by a stopwatch - and often houses them in relative isolation on the road.

Some critics say he is more than sheltering. They say he is paranoid.

He coached the United States basketball team at the Summer Olympic Games in Seoul - the bronze medalists, the first American team to conclusively lose the gold (as opposed to the 1972 team that wound up with silver in a controversial game against the Soviets).

Some critics say he ignored offers of assistance and assembled a flawed team. He has denied it and has said he would do it all again.

Two rhymes

John Thompson, 47, is black, with an exclusively black team at a predominantly white school. Over the years, he has seen and heard both subtle references to his color and the most blatantly racist slurs. If it hurts, he doesn't show it.

"To be nobody but myself - in a world which is doing its best, night and day, to make you everybody else - means to fight the hardest battle which any human being can fight, and never stop fighting."

That passage from e.e. cummings, says George Raveling, basketball coach at the University of Southern California, is one of Thompson's favorite quotes.

Raveling also was one of Thompson's assistants at the Summer Olympic Games at Seoul. "I've heard John say, and I think it's true, how amazed he is that in America, supposedly founded on individual freedoms, people want to deny him the right to be who he is. He dares to be different in a world of sameness. That, more than anything, is why I respect this man."

Two rhymes, say those who have known John Thompson well and long, reflect what drives him.

One was sung to him in childhood by his mother:

You can do anything you think you can.

It's all in the way you view it.

It's all in the start you get, young man.

You must feel you are going to do it.

The other is a verse from The Ladder of St. Augustine by Henry Wadsworth Longfellow:

The heights by great men reached and kept

were not attained by sudden flight.

But they, while their companions slept,

were toiling upward in the night.

Thompson has seen professional educators overlook potential in others - in himself - and he is a professional educator.

From Charles Smith to Alonzo Mourning and everyone in between, his   players aren't attending Georgetown for the sole purpose of winning   basketball games.

The Rev. Edward Glynn, now president of St. Peter's College in Jersey City, N.J., was Georgetown's faculty representative to the NCAA early in Thompson's tenure.

"From Day One," Glynn recalls now, "he was dedicated to making sure his players would leave school with more than the ability to shoot a basketball.

"He'd tell them there are too many people hanging around street corners with nothing but their newspaper clippings, heroes in high school or college and nothing after that."

Life after Georgetown

Raveling and Thompson have known each other since 1957, when Raveling was a student at Villanova. "What you find in John Thompson," says Raveling, "is a person who doesn't see his responsibility to his players confined to the basketball court. What I mean is that while most people might look at it as a basketball court he sees it as a classroom, a place where he can teach them lessons more valid, more important, than blocking shots and making the outlet pass.

"So many people criticize him, but we really have to ask ourselves, isn't this what we want for our own children? Wouldn't we want someone like him to teach our children?

"A lot of the way he is is that he is at peace with himself. He has been able to answer two most relevant questions: 'Who am I and what am I capable of being?' He knows who he is and he understands what he is capable of being. John sets his own standards. Be they right or wrong, they're his," Raveling says, "and he should be respected, not ridiculed, for establishing them."

For a few of his players - Patrick Ewing, Reggie Williams, Sleepy Floyd, Michael Graham and others - life after Georgetown meant professional basketball. For Ewing in particular, it meant millions of dollars and guaranteed stardom in the National Basketball Association.

It could have meant the same for Graham. He, too, had that gossamer quality of potential. But Thompson said Graham was wasting his time at Georgetown.

As a freshman in 1983-84, Graham was a major factor in the Hoyas' national championship season. Nevertheless, Thompson dropped him from the team the following season.

Graham wasn't measuring up to Thompson's academic standards, the coach said, even though Graham had met Georgetown's and the NCAA's. In the long run, Thompson said, he would have been hurting Graham by permitting him to continue playing.

Graham left Georgetown, transferred to the University of the District of Columbia, sat out the obligatory season, then left without playing a game there, without earning a degree. He was drafted by the NBA's Seattle SuperSonics and never signed a contract or played for them or anyone else in the NBA.

Today he is earning less than $10,000 playing for the Rochester (Minn.) Flyers, his fourth team in three seasons in the Continental Basketball Association.

Graham will not talk publicly about Georgetown or Thompson.

Glynn remembers an evening midway during the 1974-75 season, Thompson's third as Georgetown's coach.

"He'd lost a game up in Fairfield (Conn.)," Glynn said. "He hadn't brought along one of his star players because of academics and wasn't starting another one because he'd skipped some classes. John told me, 'I may not be able to keep my values and be a successful coach, but if I have to make a choice, I'm going to keep my values.' "

'no exceptions'

Hoya Paranoia is a headline writer's dream, and it has its genesis in fact - Thompson's zealous protectiveness of his players and his program.

His team practices are closed to everyone. On the road, the team often stays in out-of-the-way lodgings, sometimes outside the city in which they are playing.

At the annual Big East media day at the Grand Hyatt Hotel in New York, the schedule calls for two one hour sessions. The coaches meet with the print media, the players with the electronic media. Then they switch for the second hour.

Eight of the teams adhere to that schedule. Georgetown does not.

Georgetown's players stay with Thompson, grouped around him at his table. If people want to talk to Charles Smith, they must do it with Thompson at his side.

After each game, the Hoyas' media guide points out, "the Georgetown locker room will be open for 15 minutes to the press. Precisely at the end of the 15-minute period, the locker room will be closed and no more interviews will take place."

Thompson's post-game news conferences last 10 minutes, concurrent with the players' interviews, "and after that period the coach will not be available to the press. There will be no exceptions to this procedure."

Thompson was on the Archbishop Carroll (Washington D.C.) High School team. He would spend hour upon hour in neighborhood pickup games practicing his 15-foot jump shot, refusing to pass to the other kids on the team, ignoring them, working on the shot until the rest of them quit and went home.

After his two seasons as backup center to Bill Russell on a pair of Boston Celtics championship teams, he was left unprotected in the 1966 NBA expansion draft. He was claimed by the Chicago Bulls and wooed by the New Orleans Buccaneers of the new rival ABA. He knew he wouldn't have been in control of his destiny, he said, so he turned them both down and came home.

In his first coaching job, at St. Anthony's (now All Saints) High School in Washington, D.C., his teams played highly physical, full-court-defense games from start to finish. More than 20 years later, Georgetown plays the same in-your-face game.

Red Auerbach was Thompson's coach with the Celtics. Thompson, Auerbach said recently, "is the way he is because he doesn't want people to get too close to him. H e picked that up from me and Russell - take control, stay in control, put everyone else on the defensive."

He is, by his mere existence, a black role model. But while others - from Martin Luther King to Jesse Jackson - have preached change through social programs and legislation, Thompson's message is that the elimination of racism can best be achieved by eliminating poverty.

"I think more change has come about because of economics," he told the Washington Post last August, "because people totally disregard color barriers if you have economic value. Put yourself in a position of power where you create a need for yourself that has an economic effect on somebody. The world is not black or white as much as it is green."

That he is black and the team is black spawns criticism that race is a determining factor in Thompson's recruitment process. He rejects the idea out of hand. "I don't know of any white player who qualified to play on my teams that I've turned down," he says, and his supporters say Thompson does recruit white players and doesn't discriminate against them.

"I'm not going to demean myself by trying to explain myself and justify myself," Thompson says. "I'm not going to do that because some ignorant person said I'm prejudiced. I'm not interested in apologizing for being a black man. I'm as proud as I can be of that."

His critics also point to Thompson's unwillingness to schedule games against other area schools - George Washington, American, UDC, Howard - which might benefit financially with a game against Georgetown.

When the Rev. Timothy Healy, president of Georgetown, once suggested a game against George Washington, a crosstown rival, Thompson rejected the idea, saying GW's fans had shouted racist remarks at Ewing. Healy didn't push the matter.

But others accept Thompson's public explanation.

"He plays enough tough games in the Big East and one or two intersectional games with schools like LSU and Texas-El Paso," said coach Ed Tapscott of American, which was dropped from the Georgetown schedule two years ago. "A local game would be just another tough, emotional game and he doesn't need another game like that. If he beats American or George Washington or Howard, so what? He's supposed to. But if he loses, all of a sudden it's, 'What happened?'

"He's not discriminating," Tapscott said. "Effective scheduling is a part of coaching. When one has the advantage, one must press it. John does it. Every coach does what's best for his school, for his team. He's just a bigger target than everyone else - literally as well as figuratively."

'I'm going to leave him alone'

Under Thompson, Georgetown's image has become one of a street-wise, street-tough team. In the motion picture *Colors*, one of the gang members wears a Georgetown jacket. The Hoyas have engaged in their share of on-court fights.

During a nationally televised game last season, a melee broke out between Georgetown and Pittsburgh players. Former Seton Hall coach Bill Raftery, broadcasting the game on CBS, said over the air during the brawl: "John Thompson has to control his team. There are too many incidents over the years."

Thompson says he opposes fighting but points out that Georgetown plays an "aggressive" game. "We cover the full court for 40 minutes and that brings about and creates frustrations in ourselves and in other people at times."

Healy acknowledges the team's negative image and Thompson's adversarial relationship with the media, but explained in the Washington Post interview: "He runs a large program. He's got guys doing things very well. The things he doesn't do well strike me as so much less important than the things he does well. I'm going to leave him alone."

Thompson runs one of the most successful basketball programs in the nation. Because of it, he earns perhaps half-a-million dollars a year.

He is a coach, he runs a summer basketball camp, he endorses Nike athletic products, he has his own local television program, he is a highly sought-after and highly paid speaker (ProServ, the sports marketing group that represents him, says Thompson does about a half-dozen such appearances a year at about $15,000 apiece) and he lives in a house given to him by Georgetown alumni.

'this is what we want to be'

It was early in the 1974-75 season, Thompson's third as head coach of the Hoyas, one which would culminate in Georgetown's first trip to the NCAA Tournament since 1943.

He had inherited a team which, the year before he arrived, had won three of 26 games. This season, it had won seven of its first nine. But Thompson was not happy.

His players were required to sign a book verifying they had attended all their classes. His top scorer, Jonathan Smith, had signed - but he had cut some classes. When Thompson found out, he benched his star player without explanation.

Georgetown lost six consecutive games. The predominantly white student body was in an uproar.

During one game, a bedsheet was unfurled. It read: "Thompson The N----- Flop Must Go."

The next day, The Rev. Robert J. Henle, then the president of Georgetown, called a news conference and apologized to Thompson. Then Smith revealed at the news conference why he had been pulled from the starting lineup. He supported his coach.

Felix Yeomans, then the youngest player on the team, followed Smith to the microphone and listed what Thompson had done for him and for each of his teammates.

"If this is what it is to be a n----- flop," Yeomans concluded, "this is what we want to be."

Georgetown won 11 of its next 12 games, including the championship of the East Coast Athletic Conference (forerunner of the Big East Conference), and was invited to its first NCAA tournament in 32 years.

Bill Stein is the athletic director at St. Peter's College in Jersey City, N.J. He was one of Thompson's assistants at Georgetown during 1972-82. They also were teammates and roommates on the road at Providence College.

"John recruits only certain types of people," Stein says. "I know he has refused to go after players who wound up as All-Americans. Whether someone is white or black has nothing to do with it. Whether a person can fit into his program, into the kind of style he wants to play, that's what matters.

"People can make a big deal about how he's a black coach with an all-black team. A white coach with an all-white team, that's acceptable. Nobody thinks much about it. A white coach with a black team, they'd say, 'What a great guy!' "

Thompson knew, even before Georgetown won the NCAA title in 1984, that one question would inevitably arise - how he felt about being the first black coach to win a national championship. His answer was cool, reasoned, but not without a tinge of bitterness.

"When you think about it," he said, "the question is insulting. What is implied by the question is a great big blank before the first one came along. And that's a lie. Plenty of other black coaches could have won an NCAA national championship if they had ever had the opportunity. It's not the brains and talent that were missing until I came along. Those have always been there."

When he recruited Ewing, Thompson knew Patrick's mother was interested in academics first. They spent the better part of an hour in the Ewing household discussing the subject.

Then Patrick spoke up. He asked about the social life in Washington, D.C.

"With your schoolwork and the athletics," Thompson replied, "you won't have much time for a social life."

Patrick's mother made up her mind. Her son would attend Georgetown.

Mary Fenlon

It happened in the early 1980s, as Georgetown was emerging as a national power. The season and the tournament were over. The team was returning home.

In the rear of the bus, several players were carousing. From the darkness, one voice floated toward the front: "I guess this means we don't have to see you tomorrow, Miss Fenlon."

Mary Fenlon, seated beside Thompson, turned and replied: "The basketball season is over, but you're still freshmen. If you want to be sophomores, you'll be there tomorrow."

The bus fell silent for the rest of the ride.

When Thompson took over at Georgetown, three assistant coaching positions were open. He filled two of them with assistants to work on basketball. But the first person he hired was Mary Fenlon, academic coordinator. She had taught English and Latin at St. Anthony's when he coached there.

"She was a teacher, not a temporary mother or guardian," Thompson said in the Georgetown media guide, "and she got the students to do what they were supposed to do in school without the pretense of being overly affectionate with them."

At Georgetown, she is the players' tutor, their confidant. They trust her implicitly. She declines all interviews, saying politely that they "would impair my relationship with the students."

She doesn't call them players.

She also rides herd on Thompson. "If I start to interfere with the players' studies," he says, "she will let me know."

She has as much say as Thompson about who goes on road trips and who stays home to improve grades. Thompson says she also is his alter ego, his conscience. At all games, home and away, she sits on the end of the bench. She was there, too, in Seoul, at the Summer Olympic Games.

Under NCAA rules, a coach is permitted to take only full-time assistants on recruiting trips to screen and assess prospects. John Thompson takes Mary Fenlon.

Since Thompson took over as head coach, 53 of 55 basketball players who have played four years at Georgetown - 96 percent - have graduated.

In all, 67 students have played basketball at Georgetown in the Thompson era. Ten transferred to other schools and two dropped out. That reduces the graduation rate of the school's basketball players under Thompson to 79 percent.

Overall, about 70 percent of each year's entire entering freshman class graduate from Georgetown within four years, and about 80 percent eventually receive a Georgetown degree.

The NCAA said that in a recent survey of all Division I-A private schools (those major institutions such as Georgetown without Division I football programs), the graduation rate of all entering basketball players was 60 percent, the graduation rate of non-athletes 56.7 percent.

The numbers - even the discussion of them - annoy Thompson. Athletes, he says, should not be looked upon as somehow different.

"We have an educational problem in this country," he once said when the subject of basketball players' grades arose, "and I'm sick and tired of people focusing in on athletes as if that's the only place there's a problem. Athletics just reflect a small part of our society.

"The kids that we have that are participating in athletics come out of society as a whole. I'm sick about all this bull about athletics being looked at educationally. That's a bunch of hypocrisy. It's easy for people to discuss athletics."

Thompson recalled a television program he had seen in which educators were discussing whether a student with a 2.0 grade-point average in his school should be allowed to play basketball.

"Big debate!" Thompson snorted. "All these people from academic circles. I said to myself, 'Maybe I'm wrong, but I think there are other kids in educational systems who are having problems.'

"Personally, I think the athlete is fortunate. People focus in on him because of the public interest in him. Some little kid who doesn't play anything and doesn't have a 2.0, nobody gives a damn whether he has one."

Loyalty

When Thompson arrived at Georgetown in 1972, there wasn't much interest in the basketball team. The Hoyas had had only one winning season in the past five. More to the point, Maryland had a virtual lock on the Washington, D.C., media.

At the time, Thompson was Georgetown's best resource - a local star high school player, a member of two Boston Celtics championship teams and a coach at St. Anthony's.

He personally sold the Georgetown basketball program. He told Bill Carpenter, then the general manager at local television station WTTG, "Come with us now, because we'll be good some day and we won't forget where we started."

WTTG began televising the Hoyas' games. There was little viewer or sponsor support. Some station executives considered dumping Georgetown.

Carpenter stayed with it. Georgetown has since turned aside more lucrative offers and has stayed with WTTG.

"Loyalty," says Betty Endicott, WTTG's current general manager, "is one of John Thompson's strong suits."

Dennis Donaldson, an assistant basketball coach at the University of South Florida, saw Thompson's sense of loyalty in action as an assistant during the selection process for the U.S. Olympic basketball team.

"John was kind of hurt that a few players he would have liked to try out for the team stayed away because they thought it might hurt their pro careers, how their stock might go down (in contract talks because of poor performances), that they might get hurt or something.

"Like Derrick Chievous (from Missouri, now with the NBA's Houston Rockets) and Gary Grant (from Michigan, now with the Los Angeles Clippers)," Donaldson said. "There were seniors there who weren't going to make the team, who everyone knew weren't going to make the team, but John wanted them around just to help their pro careers.

"There were guys who pretty much knew they didn't have a chance (to be selected to the Olympic team) but John was so honored that they had been willing to come to the Trials that he gave them an extra shot at making it. He kept them past the first cut.

"I think what he was doing was looking to make them look better in everyone else's eyes, maybe to look better to their agents, to the media. John was trying to help them along in life. Fennis Dembo (out of Wyoming, now with the Detroit Pistons) was one for sure," Donaldson said. "He had a lot of hype coming out and was disappointing in the Trials. John told me, 'I'm not going to cut him early. I'm keeping him around. He thought enough to come here, to put the pro stuff aside, I'll help him out.' John's got some very interesting thought processes. They run a lot deeper than most people's."

Dwayne Schintzius likewise saw a softer side of Thompson. When the 7-foot-2 University of Florida center first showed up at the Trials, he was out of shape, overweight.

"A lot of coaches might have just gotten rid of me at the first cut. But he sat me down, told me I had potential, told me he liked me and that I should go home, work on my game, lose a few pounds and come back."

He did, dropping about 20 pounds. Thompson then worked with Schintzius on his game and on his attitude, and put the former Brandon High School star on the U.S. Select team that made a six-game tour of Europe in June. Schintzius survived to the final series of cuts.

"I can't believe how much I learned from him," Schintzius said. "I knew I wasn't going to make the team, but he was very fair, gave me a very fair shot."

After the United States lost 82-76 to the Soviet Union in the Olympic semifinals, Thompson bore the brunt of the criticism because he had selected a feisty, defense-oriented team similar to those he has assembled at Georgetown. He should have selected more outside shooters, the critics complained.

The only pure shooting guard, Hersey Hawkins, was injured and missed the Soviet game. And Danny Manning, one of the U.S. team's acknowledged stars, spent most of the game on the bench in foul trouble. He didn't score a point.

"The things that were done were things that we thought were in the best interest of what we were trying to accomplish," Thompson said the day after the game. "I think if I had to do it over again, every player I selected I would select again, every staff member, everything that we decided to do. You make decisions, and then you have to go with those decisions."

Stein, an assistant coach (along with Raveling) at the Olympics, said the Americans "played as well as they could have. We just had a bad game. The guys were a little tight. Our boys had played 16 games together. The Russians played something like 120. They'd been together six years with one change in personnel.

"If we played those guys 10 times, we'd beat them seven or eight (times)," Stein said. "Too much was made of one game."

Raveling said: "I think there were a lot of personal prejudices - as opposed to racial prejudices - exhibited before, during and after the Olympics. One writer told me not long after that there were some writers rooting against the U.S. team because Thompson was the coach. There's a sickness in that, that someone could actually root against his own country because of the composition of a coaching staff. No one should dislike anyone that much."

John Thompson is a 6-foot-10, 300-pound bear of a man, his countenance generally more contemplative than menacing. But perhaps because of the way he covets his private life, his insular program, and because of his size and blackness, he is sometimes characterized as a villain.

"People are just jealous of him," Auerbach, president of the Celtics and long a friend of the Georgetown coach, said earlier this month. "I don't care what anybody says, John Thompson is a dedicated guy who really cares about people, about the players who play basketball for him. Whether they become pros or not, they've got the basics to be successful in life."

"I'm not going to win many popularity contests," John Thompson once said. "I don't have to explain myself. I don't do things for other people. The people who know me know the way I am.

"I think sometimes my friends feel they have to explain or apologize for me. That's unfortunate. I don't see the need for that, but I feel affectionate toward them for doing it."

(December 26, 1988)

John Thompson announced his resignation as Georgetown's head coach on Jan. 8, 1999 after 27 seasons during which he compiled a 596-239 record. Under him the Hoyas made 24 consecutive postseason appearances. On Oct. 1, 1999, he was elected to the Naismith Memorial Basketball Hall of Fame.

Nine

'Hockey player'

TAMPA - Her name was Miss Cunningham and she taught at King Edward Public School in Sault Ste. Marie, Ontario. One of her pupils was a precocious 8-year-old from the West End, the Italian part of the Canadian town.

"She was 5-foot-2 by 5-foot-2. I never saw anything like it," Phil Esposito recalled. "She made me grab my ankles once and knocked me across the a-- with a yardstick 'cause I was such a terror.

"Y'know how teachers always ask, 'What do you want to be when you grow up?' Kids would say doctors, lawyers, nurses. Me, I'd go, 'Hockey player.' So she said, 'That's fine, but what do you want to do for a living?' "

" 'Hockey player.'

"It got to a point where she called my folks to school and told them, 'Your son will not answer the question.' My dad said, 'What's the question, Phil?' I said, 'She wants to know what I want to be. I told her. Hockey player.

"My dad looked at Miss Cunningham and said, 'What's wrong with that?' She said, 'You can't do that for a living.'

" 'Why not? If that's what he wants to be, what's wrong with that?' And she said, 'That's just not a profession for a man. It's a boy's game.'

" 'And he said, 'If my son wants to be a hockey player and that's his dream, why should you take it away from him?'

"I never forgot that. I never got bothered again and I always said it. 'Hockey player.' "

From ice to office

He spent 18 years playing in the National Hockey League with the Chicago Blackhawks, the Boston Bruins, the New York Rangers. Eight-time all-star center. Five-time NHL scoring champion. Twice its Most Valuable Player. Inducted into the Hockey Hall of Fame.

He moved from the ice to the broadcast booth, then to the Rangers' front office as their general manager. If he had a long-range plan for the team, it was never apparent to his bosses. Players came and went with mind-boggling rapidity. In 1989, after three seasons, the Rangers fired him. But the team he assembled won the 1990 Patrick Division championship, its first division title since 1942.

Esposito was wealthy. He owned a piece of several businesses ... a travel agency, a home/lawn care service and others. But when NHL training camps convened last autumn, the fire flared anew. It lit the way to Tampa Bay. On Dec. 6, against enormous odds, Phil Esposito won an NHL expansion franchise. The Tampa Bay Lightning will debut in 1992.

"There was always somebody who could skate faster or hit a ball farther. But in the long run, Phil used to beat everybody," said Pat Nardini, a science teacher at St. Mary's, a Sault Ste. Marie high school. He and Espo grew up together. "He had a knack. If he'd never done something before, he'd do it one time and before you knew it he was beating you at it."

"That's the way I've always been," Esposito said. "I was like that as a kid. I remember building these clubhouses, see, and if we didn't have any nails, I'd use rope. If we didn't have any hinges and couldn't steal 'em, I'd improvise with a piece of cardboard."

He was the neighborhood leader. He formed the local gang, the Skulls. There was Phil and his kid brother Tony, their cousin Danny DiPietro, and Lou Nanne and Nicky Kucher and Donnie Muscatello and a few other guys.

They all wore black leather jackets.

"We didn't do anything except rob gardens, steal carrots, tomatoes, celery. We didn't need it. It was just the idea of breaking into people's gardens I remember Danny, he was three years younger than me, he got beat up real bad. So I said, 'Let's go.' And me and Tony and Nicky and Donnie, we went and got the guy, got him in the laneway (alley) and held him down and I said to Danny, 'Pay him back.'

"Actually," said Danny, now a foreman at Algoma Steel in Sault Ste. Marie, "I was probably looking for trouble. Besides, I knew I had a lot of backup."

Life in the Soo

Sault Ste. Marie … everyone calls it "the Soo" … sits in south-central Ontario, 300 miles north of Detroit. It is still very much a small-town collection of ethnic neighborhoods.

When he was growing up there, Phil Esposito played fast and loose with life.

He and his buddies, especially Gino Cavicchiolo, would stand on the corner and wait for a car to come to a stop on the icy streets, then they'd grab the rear bumper, sit down and slide for a block or two.

The Esposito and DiPietro houses sat back-to-back across an alley. "The boys, they were little bootleggers, Phil and Tony and my son," said Joyce DiPietro, Danny's mother. "In those days the Italian people all made wine. There was a window (where Phil's grandparents stored the wine) and they put Danny through because he was the smallest. He'd fill up the bottles and pass them out to Phil and Tony, and they'll all go and sell them on the other end of town."

"Sell 'em to drunks in the street," Esposito said.

Then there was the DiPietro garage. "That gang of ours, we could attract girls," said Donnie Muscatello, now an executive at Algoma Steel. "They used to get lured into this garage. Nothing major happened, but we used to have some fun in there."

Tony Esposito laughed at the memory. "We didn't know what to do when we got them in there. When you're 10, 12 years old and you get a kiss, hey it's a big deal, right?"

Phil and Tony were teen-agers when Teresa ("Terri is fine," she said) was born. "Phil was more like a father than an older brother," said Terri Shelleby, an office worker at Algoma. "By the time I was 5, he was out of the house and playing hockey."

When she was an infant … Phil was 15 and Tony 14 … the boys put her in the back seat of the family car. That neither of the boys had a driver's license was inconsequential. "We went cruising the main drag looking for girls," Phil said, and Tony added: "When you had a car, all the girls wanted to go for a ride. We had to improvise. We had to babysit, but we didn't want to ruin the whole night."

Pat and Frances Esposito, out at the movies, got home first. Pat kicked his older son around the block, literally.

Out, or into Algoma

If you didn't find a way out of the Soo, you probably wound up at Algoma Steel. Pasquale Esposito ... everyone called him Pat ... did.

"My dad played a little hockey," Phil said. "He got kicked out of it. He was 13 or so and got into a fight and hurt a guy real bad and got suspended for a year and never went back. He had to go to work 'cause his mother died and his father sort of went on the skids. So him and his brothers, they went into the mill."

But Pat always loved hockey, and if his sons wanted to play it, fine.

"He stuck up for me a lot," Espo said. "I remember one time, I was 14 and playing against bigger kids. There was this guy, Harry Scott, we used to get into fights all the time, and I was coming around the net and he flattened me. I went after him and he hit me four or five good shots. Knocked me silly. My father came down from the stands and grabbed Harry, yanked him over the boards and gave him a left and said, 'You ever touch my son again, I'll kill you!'

"He was a tough guy, my dad. Never played with us all that much. But he worked hard. And when he got home, the food better be on the table. We ate every night at 5:15, like clockwork. Then we'd have to go to the store for a six-pack of Pepsi. Every night it was like that.

"And if there was hockey on TV, he'd make pizza or we'd have popcorn. We were always eating and drinking Pepsi. He was a foodaholic. My God, would he eat. Nobody could keep up with him. He was 260, 265. Almost 6 foot. His nickname was Bushel. He had a huge chest, big, big forearms and hands.

"By 10 o'clock we'd pack it in, have a sandwich before we went to bed. Always had to eat something. 'You guys hungry?' 'Yeah.' 'Okay, let's eat. Fran ... ' "

Frances Esposito was a big part of her boys' hockey indoctrination. The basement became a rink when Phil was 9 and Tony 8.

"My father wore these big wool socks at the steel plant," Phil said. "We'd get his socks and tie 'em in a ball. My mom would wax the linoleum and get big flannel diapers and we'd fold 'em over three or four times and tie them on our kneecaps. Then Tony and I, on our hands and knees, we'd bat the sock around. We'd ask mom to play goal. It was Tony and me against each other but shooting at the same net. Like one-on-one playground basketball. Mom would get socks in the face, or she'd make a save and I'd go flying in for the rebound and we'd pile up on mom."

Pasquale Esposito died of heart failure in May 1984, Frances of the same cause 13 months later. Phil still blames himself, at least a little, for his father's death. "If I'd gotten my dad out of the Soo a little sooner to see doctors in Toronto or New York …" His voice trailed off. "When I finally got him to Massachusetts, the doctor said, "You need a bypass.' He wouldn't do it. He had a stroke at 59 from diabetes he never knew he had." Five years later, he died.

School was secondary

Hockey came before school for Phil Esposito. "I was an awful student," he said. "I could not understand why I was studying Latin in high school. St. Mary's was a Catholic school, all boys. I went there after I got kicked out of Sault Collegiate, the co-ed high school. I used to …" Esposito grimaced. "It's embarrassing. I used to do some crazy things.

"I'd undo the girls' bras. Get behind and pop 'em. I got so good at it I could do it one-handed. It helped when I got to be about 17," he cackled. "Isn't that awful? I did stupid things like that."

A French teacher threw chalk at Esposito in frustration. He threw it back at her. The basketball coach chewed him out. He hit the coach in the head with the ball. He got into a scrap with the principal "and the next thing I knew," Phil said, "I was going to St. Mary's."

By the 12th grade, Esposito was in Sarnia, across the border from Port Huron, playing Junior B hockey, getting paid $10 a week plus $17.50 in room and board. His father was sending him an extra $10 a week because he was going to school.

"We went on a road trip and got back at 4 in the morning and the next morning I had an English exam," Esposito said. "I fell asleep in the classroom. After the exam was over, the sister woke me up. I asked if I could take it over. She said, 'No, it's too late. Sign your paper and hand it in.' So I wrote on it … don't forget, it's an English paper … 'I don't know nothing,' and signed my name.

"The principal called me a hockey bum and I said, "Sister, with all due respect to you and your (nun's) habit, you can take your school and stick it.' And I walked out and never went back."

He didn't tell his father for three months, until Pat showed up for a tournament. All Pat said was: "It's your life. Do what you've got to do … but if you don't make hockey, be prepared to spend the rest of your life in the mill. That's where you're going this summer.'

"By then he was a foreman. He put me in the open-hearth furnaces, 11 at night to 7 in the morning. That's no job for any human being. If he hadn't made it so tough, maybe I wouldn't have made it in hockey."

Angelo Bumbacco owned a sporting goods store in the Soo. "He gave me my first pair of skates," Esposito said. "He gave me sticks, gloves, skates and stuff when my father couldn't afford it."

"Phil was a quick learner," Bambucco said. "He excelled as a leader. The only problem was, once you put him on the ice to play, you couldn't get him off. We had to hook him off to make line changes."

'And you used to be my idol'

He spent his first NHL game, Oct. 20, 1963, on the Blackhawks' bench in Montreal. Halfway through the second one, four nights later in Detroit, coach Billy Reay sent him out on the ice.

"I lined up next to Gordie Howe. I'm looking around me. 'Jeez, Gordie Howe. Bobby Hull. Glenn Hall. What am I doing on the ice with these guys?'

"The puck drops and two seconds later, Howe gives me an elbow in the teeth (he still carries the scar from that). I swung my stick at him. We go into the penalty box and I lean over to Howe and say, 'And you used to be my idol.' He looks at me and says, 'What did you say?' 'Uh, nothing, Mr. Howe.'

"To this day, we tell that story at banquets. From that day on, we were friends. He told me he used to test every rookie and if they didn't come back at him, he owned them. 'But you came back at me, kid.' "

Being traded by Chicago to Boston after the 1967 season didn't bother Esposito. He and Reay didn't get along. But the trade to the Rangers after the 1974-75 season, "that hurt the most," Phil said. "I loved Boston and they liked me. They did it because they felt it was best for the organization. I think they were right, but it took me 4½ years to get over it.

"That was my biggest disappointment, that and not winning the Stanley Cup with the Rangers in '79. We should have, but we had too many young guys who liked to party. They didn't get their rest, that's why we lost and they'll pay for it the rest of their lives because they're out of hockey, all of them, and they'll never have a chance to win the Stanley Cup."

Esposito won two of them with the Bruins, in 1970 and '72. The next year, he blew out a knee as the Rangers knocked Boston out of the playoffs.

When the Bruins' season ended, Esposito was in traction in Massachusetts General Hospital.

"The team was having a break-up party in Bobby Orr's bar across the street," said Derek Sanderson, a teammate back then, now a Bruins television broadcaster. "About eight of us went to see Philly. When it's time to leave, he says, 'Gee, guys. I wish I could go with you.' Stupid statement to make. A couple of guys go down the hall and distract the floor nurse and the rest of us wheel him out of the room and into the elevator. We had to rip out a railing to get the bed out of the building. We wheeled him across the street and up the steps into the bar ... and Phil says, 'Gimme a Bud.' "

Sanderson said Esposito was "responsible for helping me as a player. He was the wily old veteran, but he'd never let you get down as a youngster, and he never believed in keeping his knowledge to himself.

"Even better, he was fun-loving and spontaneous. He instigated everything, had a hand in everything, but he never got caught. It was always, 'Hey, let's do this,' and then he'd back off."

He was spontaneous enough to leave an autograph session when a woman asked for a signature for her young son, a Bruins fan suffering from cerebral palsy, and to get a hockey stick, get half the team to sign it and to deliver it to the boy in the hospital.

And he was spontaneous enough at 19 to wake up a girlfriend at 7 in the morning ... he was on the way to a game in Saint Catharines ... and propose. Phil and Linda were married a year later, in 1962, and had two daughters, Carrie, now 22, and Laurie, 24. But Phil and Linda Esposito were divorced after 16 years.

Phil and Donna Esposito have been married for 12 years and have a 5-year-old daughter, Cherise. Their house in Bedford, N.Y., is up for sale. They plan to move to the Tampa Bay area.

Quit? Never!

"Craig Patrick (the Rangers' coach in 1981) afforded me one of my greatest thrills, allowing me to announce my retirement and then play my final game. My father came to that game," Esposito said.

"He said, 'Why are you quitting?' I told him, 'I'm not quitting; I'm retiring. I don't quit.' He said, 'You could still play.' I said, 'Dad, I'll be 40 in a month. What am I doing? I don't want to be a bum.' I wanted to go out like DiMaggio, not like Willie (Mays).

"To this day people still say I could've still played. It wouldn't have been worth it. But you know what's worth it? This is, having this team, this brand-new baby," Esposito said of the Lightning. "All the aggravation, all the grief, the worrying, the not being home for weeks at a time trying to pull this thing together. I feel like I'm on top of the world."

(December 16, 1990)

∼ Phil Esposito was founder, part-owner and general manager of the Lightning when the franchise was awarded to Tampa Bay in 1990. By the time it began playing in 1992 he no longer had a share of the team. When it was sold in 1998, new owner Art Williams fired Esposito. In 1989 he did hockey commentary for FOX television in Los Angeles. The following season he became the Lightning's radio analyst for home games. He also is the team's vice president for corporate relations. The Lightning won the Stanley Cup in 2004. A statue of Esposito standing in front of the Amalie Arena, the team's home ice, was unveiled December 31, 2011 ∼

Ten

Stallings' long walk home

Once in a while, he said, he has second thoughts. Then Gene Stallings thinks about John Mark and knows he has made the right decision. Alabama football will go on without him.

John Mark Stallings is 34 now, Gene and Ruth Ann's only son. He has been by his father's side on one football field or another almost since he could walk, sort of an unofficial head trainer.

And when Gene Stallings, 61, announced a week and a half ago, minutes after Alabama's 24-23 victory over Auburn, that this would be his last season as head coach, his son stood by, his face an amalgam of pride and pain.

"He's just getting worn down," Stallings said. "We need to get him somewhere where there is fresh air. You don't understand how (football) affects Johnny, the pressure on him when we lose."

John Mark Stallings was born with Down Syndrome, a congenital disorder characterized by moderate to severe mental retardation and slow physical development. Doctors told Gene and Ruth Ann that their son would live only a few years and, as was common in the 1960s, should be institutionalized. He wasn't. They brought him home, loved him as much as they loved his four sisters and gave him as normal a life as they could.

That life will change now. The Stallings family will move to the family ranch in Paris, Texas. "I don't think John Mark completely understands the magnitude of the decision," Gene Stallings said.

"I don't think he realizes he won't be riding in the police cars any more and won't be walking on the field with me. He'll miss it, but he'll also enjoy the fresh air and open spaces he'll have.

"It'll be bittersweet for Ruth Ann, too. She's knowledgeable about football and loves the excitement. But we've never really experienced fall together in all these years."

Probation

Stallings in 1992 guided the Crimson Tide to its first national championship since 1979, the last of Bear Bryant's six titles. He leaves an Alabama football program in a transition of sorts.

His successor will have to deal with the residue of a three-year probation the NCAA imposed in 1995 because of rules violations involving former players Antonio Langham, who signed with an agent in 1993 but continued to play, and Gene Jelks, who took an improper loan from a booster. The sanctions included the loss of 26 scholarships over three years.

"I don't think the cupboard will be bare," Stallings said. "It's in pretty good shape. We have a lot of fine young talent here already."

Without the NCAA sanctions, the first ever against Alabama, Stallings' Tide record would be 69-15-1 and he would be one win away from 70 in seven seasons, a feat not even Bryant could achieve. But part of the punishment included Alabama's forfeiting 11 games in 1993. The resulting 1-12 record was its worst since the winless 1955 season.

Stallings reportedly didn't get along with new athletic director Bob Bockrath, and Bockrath confirmed that they have had philosophical differences.

Said Auburn coach Terry Bowden: "He has earned my respect, whether he cared for it, and he should have earned everybody's. If he's retiring because it's the right time for him, I'm happy for him. If it's for other reasons, I'm disappointed. ...

"You don't go through the Auburn-Alabama rivalry without gaining at least some respect for what the other guy's going through. It's really tough at Auburn, but I have a feeling it's tougher at Alabama because of the expectations."

'I'm on the way'

In 1960 Stallings had written *Bear Bryant on Winning Football.* He was one of Bear's assistant coaches at Alabama back then. Benny Marshall, sports editor of the Birmingham News, was supposed to write it; Stallings was supposed to help him. When Marshall backed out, Stallings stepped in.

"I knew nothing about writing a book," Stallings said. "I went home that night, took out a yellow tablet and wrote down the word, 'Chapters.' Then I wrote the numbers 1 through 12. Then I called my wife in and told her, 'Ruth Ann, I'm on the way.' I'd kept every note from every staff meeting and team meeting. I knew what Bear wanted."

Nearly 30 years later, Stallings recalled, when he was coaching the Phoenix Cardinals, he received a letter. "It said, 'Dear Author, This is a letter that all you authors hate to receive. There's no longer any demand for your book. We've got about 3,000 left; we'll sell 'em to you, half price, or we'll burn 'em.'

"I wrote back, 'Burn 'em.' Then I came to Alabama and wished I hadn't."

If he wrote the book ... literally ... on Bear Bryant, and had Bear's stoop-shouldered shuffle and rich Southern drawl, Stallings still will tell you not to waste your time on comparisons. "Those of us here in Alabama love Coach Bryant and tolerate the rest of us," he said. "I understand that."

In some cases, even tolerate was too generous a word.

Legend has it that Bryant, who announced his retirement just six weeks before dying of a heart attack on Jan. 26, 1983, recommended Stallings as his successor. But Alabama went with Ray Perkins and, when he left to take the Bucs' coaching job in 1987, hired Bill Curry.

Perkins couldn't win an SEC title and, despite being a 'Bama alumnus, never won over the hearts of Tide fans. And Curry, despite winning the 1989 SEC title (before losing to Miami in the Sugar Bowl) and posting a 26-10 record, was considered an interloper from Georgia Tech, which Bryant had despised. Besides, Curry was unable to beat archrival Auburn in three tries. When he left for Kentucky, Stallings succeeded him.

Now, with a new regime running things, Stallings has decided it's time to leave. "I think they've got agendas that they want to get handled," he said. "I'm basically the only one that was left from the old regime. We have a new president, new athletic director, new provost, new compliance director, new faculty chairman of athletics.

"Sometimes, you just feel it might be best to step aside."

He said he might coach again someday, either in college or the NFL, if someone wants him. But that, Stallings added, is a big if. ""I don't think anyone's going to be knocking my door down," he said.

(December 5, 1996)

~ *Gene Stallings played offensive end and defensive back at Texas A&M, was an assistant coach at Alabama and with the NFL's Dallas Cowboys, and a head coach at Texas A&M, with the NFL's St. Louis/*

Phoenix Cardinals and Alabama. Stallings was inducted into the College Football Hall of Fame as a coach in 2010. He also is in halls of fame at Alabama, Texas, Texas A&M, and the Gator Bowl and Cotton Bowl. John Mark Stallings died August 2, 2008, of complications due to a congenital heart problem. He was 46. Bronze statues of Gene and John Mark stand together inside the entrance to the John Mark Stallings football field at Faulkner University in Montgomery, Ala. ✑

Eleven

You have to give credit where credit is due

I was staring at the bill. I can't tell you how much it was for, but I can tell you it was for a hell of a lot more than I had.

We were in Basin Street East, the late, lamented jazz joint in midtown Manhattan. She'd had too much to drink. So had I. Not that we were drunk, or even giggly, but I was a naive 20 and she was 19 and we'd never been taught that alcohol in a New York City nightclub attacks your wallet faster than it hits your reflexes.

Mr. Big Shot had borrowed dad's car for the evening and ...

Oh, great. If I can't pay the check, how am I supposed to get the Plymouth out of the parking lot?

"Umm, Carole?"

I whispered those three little words that mean so much.

"You got money?"

She did - enough for the tab and part of the parking lot, anyway. I could take care of the rest of the parking and if we took the Brooklyn Bridge home (the long-but-free way) instead of the Brooklyn-Battery Tunnel, I could actually leave the waiter some semblance of a tip instead of stiffing him altogether.

I'd had to borrow money from my date. In 1962 this was not cool. I was determined never, ever to submit to such embarrassment again.

I would get myself a credit card.

Thumbing through a magazine, I found a Diner's Club application. I filled it out, giving my correct age, my occupation (college student), my residence (living with my parents in Brooklyn; I commuted by subway to Long Island University), my income (none), and so on.

It didn't take long for Diner's Club to respond with a form letter which, in several paragraphs, advised me: *Are you serious? Get lost!*

Well, who needed Diner's Club? There were other credit card companies out there - Carte Blanche, American Express. They wouldn't mind extending me a little credit, would they?

Just to make sure, I, umm, fudged a bit on the American Express application.

No, let me rephrase that. I lied through my teeth.

Age: I added 10 years.

Occupation: I owned my own fraternity supply company. (Well, I had once made a paddle as part of my initiation into Tau Delta Phi at LIU.)

Residence: I owned my own home. (Okay, my brother and I were in the will.)

Income: I figured thirty-something-thousand sounded about right. (I did give my real bank account; I just added a zero to my balance.)

Was there anything honest in the application?

My name.

How long would it be before the vigilant American Express researchers found me out? And what would they do? Besides turning me down, I mean. Report me to the feds? To my bank? To my parents?

The card arrived a few weeks later. Unbelievable! I had slipped through the cracks of their credit check, or else they didn't care who had their card.

This was cause for celebration. I called Carole. I was going to repay her kindness by taking her to dinner, a special dinner, and if the bill came to more paper than I had in my wallet, so what? I had plastic.

Peter Luger's is one of the great steak joints in the world, maybe the greatest. Back then I knew it only by reputation. I'd never been there; I couldn't afford it; not even close.

But I'd read about it and Playboy had declared it to be one of the greats, and if Hugh Hefner said so. ...

The restaurant is in Williamsburg, a generally decrepit, dangerous part of Brooklyn. It hasn't changed much since the '60s. A member of the staff will escort you from and to your car. Fatally wounded patrons are not good for business.

I dressed for the occasion, suit and tie, and picked up Carole in the Plymouth. She, too, understood the importance of the occasion and was dressed accordingly. This was going to be special.

It was. The porterhouse was everything I imagined, the sliced tomatoes and onions perfect. The mood. The company.

he check.

I didn't even flinch at the numbers. I was a card-carrying member of American Express. With a practiced flourish, I placed it upon the check. The waiter would be suitably impressed.

"I'm sorry, sir," he said, "but we don't accept any credit cards except our own.'"

I had to borrow money from Carole to get us out of the restaurant.

She never went out with me again.

The imprint on my credit card still reads: MEMBER SINCE 62.

(July 13, 1994)

Twelve

Voices of the past

We listened to the games through their eyes and saw them with our imagination.

There might have been television then, but the picture was black and white, the screen not much bigger than a batter's glove.

Cable? That usually was bad news you signed for at the front door. Instant replay? Kids called it a do-over and the arguments went on forever.

Baseball came to us through the radio then. You didn't just hear it. You absorbed it.

And the voice coming out of the Philco, the Crosley or the Stromberg Carlson was as familiar and comfortable as the easy chair next to it.

Mel Allen, Bob Prince, By Saam, Jack Brickhouse, Russ Hodges, Harry Caray, Red Barber, Bob Elson … their names evoke voices in our minds - sepia-toned and soft-edged like daguerreotypes of our grandparents.

They could be the guy who sat next to you in the ballpark, game after game, and became your friend.

We watched the radio, stared at it, seeing subtle details. Our emotions would ebb and flow with descriptions so vivid all our senses experienced it from the best seat in the ballpark.

"Radio was the most important piece of furniture in the house," said Ernie Harwell, voice of the Tigers, retiring this season after 55 years as a broadcaster. "That was when families stayed together and they felt a loyalty not just to teams but to players.

"Now we're listening to it in cars, on headsets. Radio has a niche because of its portability to the beach, the workplace, the kitchen. Radio is with us all the time. It's background that TV can't match."

For many it is a second-rate substitute for television. "When you listen to the game on radio in your car you're sort of saying to yourself, 'Where's the TV?'" said Bob Costas, broadcaster and unabashed fan born 50 years ago when television still was grainy shades of gray. "Even when you're at the ballpark you want to see a replay."

They are a vanishing breed

Harwell's voice and a few others of an earlier era are still around - Vin Scully with the (former Brooklyn) Dodgers, Ralph Kiner with the Mets, Jack Buck with the Cardinals …

They and their contemporaries represent the final link to what baseball used to represent - stability and dependability in the decades before free agency. The world might change but our baseball team didn't.

Harwell and Scully are more a part of their teams than the interchangeable players, even stars. They're the only ones still around.

We tend to mythologize indelible moments in our minds, thinking of long-gone ballparks with their quirky outfield fences, and frankfurters slathered with mustard and served at our seat. Far less vivid are the terrible sightlines and nasty smells.

"Even when we had 16 teams we had bad players," Harwell said. "People tend to forget that. As they look back, everything's a little more golden. They don't remember the bad players. They remember the Babe

Ruths and Hank Greenbergs. Even the old players don't remember all the bad things. They remember the camaraderie, the good times."

Scully has broadcast Dodgers games since 1950, before they fled Flatbush for Los Angeles. "People will forever say to me, 'I love to hear your voice because it reminds me of when I heard it a long time ago,'" he said. "'It reminds me of summer nights in the backyard with my dad,' or fishing or something."

They are a vanishing breed, men who spoke to us before television obliterated our inner vision, before baseball's radio voices began to sound alike, talk so much more and say so much less.

"The Barbers and Scullys came up with radio," Costas said. "They had to be able to paint the picture. The attention to detail, having to describe the whole thing, was part of how these guys came along.

"The craft is different now. Even the talented guys on radio today have been influenced by having come up with television. Rarely do you hear a guy say what a player's number is or what his stance looks like or talk about adjustments in the outfield alignment. Sometimes you hear a guy call a home run and not even say where in the ballpark it went out. Like, 'Oh, that's gone.'"

'Going, going, gone!'

The home run call is a broadcaster's signature. Allen's was "Going, going, gone!" although Harry Hartman is credited with having said it first at a 1929 Reds game. They were simple yet dramatic: Harwell's "It's long gone!" Kiner's "It's gone, goodbye!" Caray's "It could be, it might be, it is. A home run!" Prince's "Kiss it goodbye!" Hodges' "Bye, bye, baby!"

Scully never has had a home run call. It is its very absence that builds the drama. "When I first started, I would follow the outfielder. I'd say, 'Long fly ball to left. Hermanski going back. ... Way back. ... To the track. ... At the wall. ... Gone!'"

Some of today's calls have something of a manufactured sound to them, like Ken Harrelson's "You can put it on the board. Eeee-yessss!" with the White Sox and Paul Olden's "Take the grand tour!" with the Rays. But they, too, carry on a tradition born in Arch McDonald's "There she goes, Mrs. Murphy!" with the Senators, and Rosey Roswell's "Open the window Aunt Minnie, here it comes!" followed by the sound of shattering glass and "She didn't make it!"

"That stuff was a little corny, but it was more acceptable then because we had a cornier view of baseball anyway," Costas said. "That was part of its charm."

It wasn't just a matter of painting a picture. They orchestrated the sound and feel of a game with pauses, letting the crowd fill in the silences. "That was part of the trick of broadcasting, not talking," said Kiner, a Mets broadcaster since their inception in 1962 and for the White Sox before that. "Letting the crowd noise carry through could dramatize the event better than we could by trying to explain it."

They also had an historical perspective, recalling some long-forgotten name or moment, putting the game aside for a while, telling a tale interrupted occasionally by a pitch. "That part of the game has changed a lot," Kiner said. "You don't have those tie-ins with the ancient history of the game."

True, said Charley Steiner, first-year Yankees broadcaster after 14 with ESPN Radio, "but we're talking about a frame of reference. We're just not old enough to have been there with Ruth and Gehrig. But we are old enough to have been there with Yastrzemski and Gibson and Musial and Koufax and Clemente. And for these (younger broadcasters) it'll be Ripken and Gwynn and McGwire and Bonds."

Today, the trap is statistics - what a batter does with runners in scoring position and fewer than two outs in a night game on the road.

"The most important thing we have to do these days as broadcasters is to learn to edit," Olden said. "We get so much material that we have to know what's important and what's not. I think it promotes a lot of extra talking because some announcers feel they have to repeat everything in those stat sheets."

And Steiner noted: "In the old days they didn't have computers and all those numbers readily available. If they did I suspect they'd have used them."

Gone, for good - they would be a laughable anachronism now - are the re-creations. In a simpler time they were a particular kind of magic.

When a broadcaster didn't accompany the team on road games, he sat in a room reading Western Union ticker tape that said sng rf or s3. What it really was, he didn't know. He decided whether the single to right was a bloop or a liner, whether Strike 3 froze the batter or had him flailing away.

And when the wire broke down, which it often did, that was when the real creativity kicked in.

"We'd make up rain delays," Kiner said. "We could talk about anything we wanted to. Or there'd be a fight in the stands, a dog on the field. It was amazing what you could do and how you did it."

With recorded crowd noise, a make-believe crack of the bat, and an imagination, we heard games so authentic that - despite the clicking of the telegraph - we willed ourselves to believe we were seeing it.

For home games we knew every nuance of the ballpark and its fans and we were there, watching Del Rice block the plate in Sportsman's Park or Lum Harris taking another pounding in Shibe Park.

We no longer see baseball our own way. If we hear the game on the radio, we know we'll see highlights on SportsCenter, televised replays from different angles and in slow-motion.

We all see it the same way.

And we leave our imagination next to the remote.

(May 17, 2002)

∾ Ernie Harwell was a broadcaster for 42 years with the Detroit Tigers. He also called games for the Brooklyn Dodgers, New York Giants, Baltimore Orioles and California Angels. He retired at the end of the 2002 season. He died May 4, 2010 of cancer. He was 92.

Ralph Kiner, a Hall of Fame slugger, played 10 Major League seasons, most of them with the Pittsburgh Pirates, before back problems forced him to retire at age 32. From 1962 to 1996 he was a full-time broadcaster for the New York Mets, then cut back to part time due to Bell's palsy. He died Feb. 6, 2014. He was 91.

Vin Scully began broadcasting Dodgers games in 1950, when Harwell left for the Giants. Scully followed the Dodgers to Los Angeles and says he plans to be in their broadcast booth for his 67th season in 2016. ∾

Thirteen

Playing his role in a made-for-TV move

MENLO PARK, Calif. - The room is small, about 10 by 15 feet. On the wall just to the right of the entrance is a huge, framed end-zone photograph of Ronnie Lott, Keith Fahnhorst, Keena Turner and Joe Montana, the four captains of the 1986 San Francisco 49ers.

Just below the photo, a television monitor is framed by stacks of videotapes. On another wall, smaller pictures, handshakes with President Bush, with Giants manager Roger Craig, with other celebrities, all of them with "To my good friend ..." inscriptions.

On a nearby table, a wire sculpture of an airborne 49er catches a pass over a badly beaten defender. Behind the sculpture, a picture window overlooks the tree-laden hills and fog-dappled sky of the northern California peninsula.

It is a sylvan setting, this executive office park, all burnished woods and polished chrome and glass, the consummate California think tank. Where else for a 57-year-old genius to retire after 10 years up the coast, in front of the 49ers' bench?

Bill Walsh was picking up some of the videotapes and books that had spilled off the shelves the night before. The phone rang. 'Nothing

99

serious," he said. "Just some things knocked over. We were lucky. The house got it worse. Some glass broken, huge cracks in the driveway. The quake wrenched the place hard enough that it threw water 10 feet out of the pool. But we're okay."

He had been at Candlestick Park Tuesday night, sitting with Giants president Al Rosen, waiting for the World Series to resume, when the ballpark began to wobble. "Amazing," he said of the earthquake. "All my years in California and I'd never seen anything even remotely like it."

Walsh sprawled angularly in an office chair. He is unable to sit still for more than a few seconds without uncrossing and recrossing his legs or stretching them or clasping and unclasping his hands behind his head.

He is, he said, totally relaxed, yet he seems ill at ease without the turbulence of an NFL game swirling around him.

It still swirls, but now it does so far below the broadcast booth where he and Dick Enberg share NBC's microphones and cameras. He appears to have made the transition from coach to commentator with remarkable ease.

Not quite.

"Thirty years," he said of his journey through college and professional coaching - California, Stanford (twice) and the Raiders, Bengals, Chargers and 49ers. "Many games. Many teams."

"It's easy to philosophize about changing careers at this stage of life, but once you do it, it's a new arena and you're in with young, bright, capable people. I don't wish I was still coaching, but it did hurt to leave it.

"There's a grieving process you go through when you leave a career. After putting together a team, establishing a whole organization, it's very difficult to leave the players, to leave something you've built and nurtured. The individuals, the lifestyle.

"All of us go through it at some stage of our life. Fortunately for me, I went through it at an earlier age than some, so there was this other career out there. But I can see how a person could reach that automatic age of 65 and be retired and then just be in an absolute state of desperation," Walsh said. "You lose your environment, friends, a scheme of living. That's been a wrenching thing.

"This job helps, but I'm all by myself. I sit alone in a hotel room, getting ready to go to a game, and say to myself, 'What the hell am I doing? Why put myself through this?' And I'm all alone out there. I mean, whatever I say, I can't say the quarterback missed the count. If I blow it, I have no one to lay it off on."

Walsh spends three or four days a week in the office, seven or eight hours a day (minus breaks for tennis) studying game tapes of the teams he will be seeing the following Sunday, memorizing names and numbers, "developing a feeling about each team, developing some thoughts and stories about experiences with them. I keep this board of notes. Late in the week, I'll be traveling and interviewing some of the players."

It was a calculated gamble by Terry O'Neil, executive producer of NBC Sports, hiring Walsh for more than $250,000 a year and making him part of the network's No.1 broadcasting team.

"They called so I decided, why not?" Walsh said. "They put on a game, took the sound off, and I did the game off the television. They liked it. Then I had to do some hard thinking, to decide whether to go ahead with it.

"It's like many things. You sit in a nice comfortable situation and say, 'Why not? Let's go for it. Why not climb Mount Everest? We'll leave tomorrow.' But once you've committed, then comes the challenge."

He is reserved, pensive, soft-spoken, very much the antithesis of CBS' resident coach-genius, flamboyant John Madden. Yet Walsh has the same credentials. What he doesn't have yet is a broadcaster's trademark - Madden's boisterous delivery or Cosell's multisyllabic condescension.

If he sounds a bit too tutorial, too technical, he nevertheless exudes a warmth in his broadcasts that rarely exhibited itself in locker rooms and press conferences. And, only six games into the season, he is still learning.

"I figure by midseason I'll be okay," he said. "I might not sound any different, but I'll feel okay. The apprehension will be gone."

On Sunday, at Stanford Stadium in Palo Alto, Walsh will get his first opportunity to analyze his former team as a broadcaster. "It's going to feel odd, working the (Patriots-49ers) game," Walsh said. "Not because of any history of antagonism. I know whatever remarks I make, I'm going to be as objective as I can be."

The 49ers were not the most gracious of teams in discussing their former coach, the man who molded them into three-time Super Bowl champions and made them rich.

When he left, when his hand-picked successor, former defensive coordinator George Seifert, ascended to the head coaching position, some players sniped at Walsh. They said he was overbearing, aloof, mysterious. And when Seifert opened training camp, Montana said, "It's like a breath of fresh air around here."

Walsh forgives them their transgressions.

"I think we had all kinds of fun as a team," he said, recalling with a laugh the times he masqueraded as a bellhop when the team bus pulled up to a Super Bowl hotel. "But, yes, I was tough, too. A coach has to be. And with me being in charge of everything, I'm sure people were anxious around me.

"So my being gone is like the principal leaving the high school for a while. There's a sense of relief. This has affected me, what I've read."

He is, he said, a victim of his own system.

"I've always stressed that if a player is injured, whoever comes in plays the best of his career and everyone else closes ranks and plays that much better. When Joe (Montana) was hurt, we'd come back with a winner as a quarterback. Matt Cavanaugh, Jeff Kemp, Steve Young. Not that they were comparable to Joe, but everyone else played better.

"When I left, they closed ranks. I waved goodbye and they waved goodbye. Now I know how tough it is on (tackle) Keith Fahnhorst. Suddenly we're all talking about Harris Barton. 'Bright young player. Can improve the position.' And there's Keith after 14 years. We wave goodbye and keep going.

"Now I'm a victim of it myself, and it hurts."

But it was time to leave. "Ten years was enough with any given team," Walsh said.

There already was speculation that he wouldn't remain as head coach for the final year of his contract. He began thinking seriously about it last Nov. 13, after the 49ers had been beaten 9-3 by the Raiders.

The following day, he met with team owner Eddie DeBartolo Jr. and suggested several options: remain as coach in 1989; step aside as coach but remain director of football operations; become a consultant; leave completely.

"By continuing on one more year, I don't know if I would have accomplished anything," Walsh said. "The last thing I wanted to be was a lame-duck coach. All I'd hear is, 'Who's going to be the new head coach?' The ideal thing was to just step away. I'd have left after 1987 if we'd won that Super Bowl - and I'm still not sure that I wouldn't have come back if we hadn't won it after '88."

He never would have been there had he not been rejected for the Bengals' top job in 1976 following eight years of coaching Cincinnati's quarterbacks and receivers. He had spent game days in a box high above the field while Bill "Tiger" Johnson, the offensive-line coach, roamed the sidelines with head coach Paul Brown. In fact, Walsh was the Bengals' offensive coordinator without the title.

"I think Paul wanted to keep things pretty much the same way - me upstairs and Bill on the field," Walsh said of Brown's decision to make Johnson the head coach. "I was hurt when he was passed over me. I didn't feel cheated, but the way Bill's career was going, I thought it was good judgment that I leave."

He was 45, and he was worried. "At that age, the odds really begin to mount whether you'll ever be a head coach." Walsh signed on as Tommy Prothro's offensive coordinator with the San Diego Chargers for a year ("He told me that eventually I'd replace him, but I'd just been through that."), then became head coach at Stanford, where he had been an assistant coach in the mid-1960s.

"If I hadn't left Cincinnati, if I hadn't come to the (West) coast, the Stanford job wouldn't have been there for me. And without that, I don't think I would have gotten the 49ers. I think maybe I was fortunate I didn't become a head coach too early."

Having apprenticed under Brown, under Prothro and under Al Davis' tutelage with the Oakland Raiders in the mid-1960s, "I was on the cutting edge of professional football," Walsh said.

Which brings us back to the "genius" business.

"Labels," Walsh said, "are usually because of appearance. I'm sure that was a big part of it. I'm proud if people respect my technical knowledge of the game. But all the rest of it, what am I going to say? No, I'm not? Yes, I am? It's like, 'When did you stop beating your wife?' I'm stuck with it."

Walsh apologized. It was time to get back to work, to slip another tape into the VCR.

Is he happy in his new job?

"Happy?" Bill Walsh gazed out his picture window. "Just look at those hills."

(October 20, 1989)

~ *Walsh, saying he missed the sidelines, left NBC after three years to return to Stanford as its head coach for three seasons. From 1999-2001 he served as the 49ers' general manager. He was elected to the Pro Football Hall of Fame in 1993. Walsh died July 30, 2007 of leukemia. He was 75. After his death the Stanford-San Jose State game was renamed the Bill Walsh Legacy Game.* ~

Fourteen

Abrupt end to a dream

SARALAND, Ala. – "Hey, you comin' tonight?"

Ronald Sims had been standing on the parched red clay along the third-base line of the baseball field, staring toward the leftfield fence and the light towers beyond.

He used to hit home runs over that fence, 325 feet down the line, curving away to 375 in straightaway center. He used to hit home runs over those 50-foot light towers a year ago when he was the star of the Satsuma High School team that won the Alabama state championship.

He walked back through the chain-link fence that separated this field from the others in the municipal park. Satsuma would be on the field that night, back in the playoffs.

He'd be there, he replied.

He'd hang around with the guys who used to be his teammates, talk with the man who just knew he had been coaching a future major-leaguer.

Ronald Sims, the brim of an Atlanta Braves cap shielding his 19-year-old face, the deep brown of his sunglasses hiding his one good eye, walked out of the park and headed home.

The seventh inning

A career has to start somewhere. Sims' began on June 20, 1988, in Bradenton, with the Braves, Atlanta's rookie team in the Gulf Coast League.

He had played first and third base at Satsuma. The Braves put him at second base. "I could do that," he said.

But he felt uncomfortable at the plate. Braves coaches had altered his batting stance. He had always had a closed stance, virtually looking over his left shoulder. The coaches had pulled his left foot back, opening the stance a bit.

His first two times up in his first professional game had been routine, one fly ball, one grounder.

Now it was the seventh inning and Napoleon Robinson of the Sarasota Dodgers was pitching his first professional inning.

Sims took one pitch for a strike, then swung and missed the second one. Robinson decided to waste a pitch, to throw a fastball outside.

As Robinson released the ball, Sims began his stride.

Twenty-one trophies, a dozen plaques

To get to Short Street, cross the Southern and the Burlington Northern railroad tracks into the wooded neighborhood known as Black Jacks. Most of the homes sit on concrete blocks. Some of them are little more than shacks. Some are boarded up. One of the abandoned homes has KKK spray-painted on a door.

Short Street is one block long, a dirt road. Jerome and Nettie Sims' blue clapboard house sits across from a water-pumping station.

Six of their seven children still live with them - Ronald, two brothers and three sisters. Derrick, 23, moved to Atlanta last year.

The Sims' front sitting room is a veritable shrine to the young man generally regarded as the premier power hitter in the Mobile area. Twenty-one trophies are clustered on a coffee table, on a credenza, on the television. A dozen plaques dot the walls.

When he started out, Ronald Sims played Peanut League baseball with the rest of the 6-year olds. Within a month he was up in the Minor League level. Within two, he was a Major Leaguer on a Dixie Youth team with some kids twice his age. But that was organized baseball.

Around the neighborhood, the rules were different. "I tried playing baseball with the big kids," he said. "Most times, they wouldn't let me. They thought I was mostly in the way. So me and the other little guys would play our own game."

Once in a while he'd go up to the big kids. "I'm better than you!" he'd tell them. "Someday I'll prove it."

By then, he said, he knew he was going to play baseball in the real major leagues.

In 1988, in 25 games as a junior at Satsuma High, he batted .455 with 12 home runs and 41 runs batted in.

"He would've made it all the way (to the major leagues). He would've made it up through the minors pretty quick because of the way he hit the ball," said Mike Szymanski, Sims' coach at Satsuma. "Ronald was the best high-school hitter I'd ever seen. He had such tremendous bat speed."

'I saw it, but I couldn't move'

As Sims stepped into Robinson's pitch, the ball sailed up and in. It slammed full force into his left eye, shattering the surrounding bones and breaking Sims' nose.

"I saw it," Sims said, "but I couldn't move."

"What happened," according to Dr. Matthew Mosteller, an ophthalmologist in Mobile who treated Sims when he returned home, "is that he lost the pupil, the iris, the lens, the vitreous humor (the colorless jelly-like substance that fills the eyeball between the retina and lens), the majority of the retina … all of this was gone. Nothing was salvageable."

"What people call an eye transplant is actually a cornea transplant. It's the equivalent of changing a watch crystal," Mosteller said. "But in this case, the entire mechanism was irretrievably damaged."

Sims lay on the ground, fully conscious and not really in pain. "It was more like a numbness that covered the whole side of my face," he said. Ice and towels were applied to the injury.

Robinson watched from the mound. "I knew it had hit him but I didn't think he got hurt that bad. I thought maybe it hit his helmet," he said. "I didn't know what happened until later on."

Sims was taken to Blake Memorial Hospital in Bradenton.

"I was lying somewhere and I heard a couple of doctors talking to themselves," he said. "They said they were going to have to take my eye out. I don't think they knew I was awake. … I didn't believe them. I thought it was just something that they could fix."

Baseball was his only option

Once he discovered just how good a baseball player he was, everything else became secondary to Ronald Sims. "He'd come to Sunday school as a young boy," said the Rev. Robert King, pastor of the Church of God Pentacostal in Saraland. "After he began to play baseball in high school, that was his world, playing ball. That was the only thing he looked forward to. He stopped coming to church."

"He wasn't much of a student," said Szymanski, his former coach. "He failed several classes. He more or less just passed enough to play every year, had to go to summer school twice just to stay eligible."

His high school athletic eligibility ran out after his sophomore year, Satsuma High principal Lee Shoquist said, because Sims turned 19 before last Sept. 1. He had about two years' worth of classes left if he wanted to earn his diploma.

Or he could try to become a professional ballplayer.

He was ignored in the June 1-3 summer free-agent draft, in part because some teams were unaware that he was draft-eligible, in part because some didn't think he was as good as he thought he was.

The Braves didn't know he could be drafted. A week later, Sims showed up at their tryout camp at the University of South Alabama at Mobile.

His high school coach's enthusiasm for Sims' skills was not universally shared.

"We thought he had some tools, some potential," said Ted Sparks, the Braves' scout who signed him. "He hit a couple of good line drives off a college pitcher who had good velocity and pretty good breaking stuff."

On June 10, Sims' 19th birthday, the Braves signed him to a professional contract. They gave him a $5,000 bonus.

"He would've been a low-round pick at best," Sparks said. "I can't say that he was major-league material. But he did have the right attitude. He wanted it bad enough."

Joe Campbell, an Alabama-based scout for the Dodgers, had seen Sims play at Satsuma. He knew Sims was available in the draft. "We drafted 60 kids," he said. "That means we felt there were 60 kids who were better than he was.

"His tools were very limited. He was a strong kid who was going to have a hard time finishing high school. ... His hands were so-so, his arm strength so-so. His running speed was a little above average. The best thing he had going for him was his bat strength. He had a real low chance of making it (to the majors).

"He was a kid who got a break when he got signed at all," Campbell said. "Five thousand dollars is a low amount to pay for anyone with promise. As a matter of fact, it's pretty high for a young man who wasn't drafted."

Breaking the news slowly

It was Rod Gilbreath, the Braves' assistant scouting director, who called Nettie, Ronald's mother, in Saraland. "It had been put to me that his eyeball had completely exploded," he said, "but I couldn't tell her that right away. I didn't want to get her into a complete state of panic."

What he told Mrs. Sims at first was that her son had been "in an accident."

"At first I thought it was like a car crash or something," she said. "Then he told me Ronald had been hit by a ball and was already in surgery and they wanted us to fly down. I thought he was just about dead."

When Jerome and Nettie Sims visited their son, she knew he wasn't prepared for the worst. "Every day I was there, I'd tell him a little bit more," she said. "I told him maybe he would lose his eye. Then I told him he'd probably lose it. ..."

Robinson, the pitcher, visited the hospital the day after the accident. Sims was still heavily sedated. "His mother and father were there," Robinson said. "They said they knew I didn't do it on purpose."

He is still with the Dodgers' rookie league team, and he thinks about the accident "only when someone brings it up, not when I'm out there pitching. ... For a couple of games I was throwing outside, trying to keep away from them. If a pitch got inside, I might worry for a second. But after a while I got over it. You start worrying about that, you're not going to be a very good pitcher."

And yes, he said, he has hit several batters since then. "In the ribs mostly. I didn't freeze or say, 'Oh, my God!' or anything like that. You don't mean to hit people … but you're going to get hit if you bat."

He never doubted his talent

As far as Ronald Sims was concerned, the Dodgers, the Braves and every other team that passed on him during the draft had made a mistake. "I never thought maybe I wasn't as good as I thought I was," he said, a convoluted way of saying he always believed he'd be a major-leaguer.

"I had my mind set on making it all the way. I wasn't going to come back home early. I wasn't going to leave until they told me to get out, and if they told me to go, I'd go around to other teams until somebody wanted me."

As far as his mother was concerned, Sims was just getting baseball out of his system, seeing how far his talents might take him. "I think he just wanted to try," she said. "If he didn't make it, well, he just wasn't going to make it. But at least he would have tried."

Shortly after the accident, Henry Aaron, the Braves' director of player development and a native of Mobile, visited Sims in Bradenton.

"Mr. Aaron promised me Ronald would always have a place in baseball with the Braves," Mrs. Sims said then.

Several days later, Sims returned home. On June 27, Mosteller examined him. "He had perfect 20-20 vision in his right eye and his left eye had no light perception," the ophthalmologist said. "When there is no light at all, and when someone is in obvious pain (caused by the extreme high pressure in the damaged eye on still-functioning nerve fibers), there obviously is no hope for any vision at all. The best thing to do is to get him out of the pain by removing the seeing parts of the eye that have been totally damaged."

Besides, he said, if the damaged parts of an eye are not removed, the good eye can begin experiencing "sympathy" problems.

On June 30 the remaining parts of Sims' left eye were removed and cosmetic surgery was performed. By October, a prosthetic device, commonly called a glass eye, was placed in the socket.

"When he first came home, he wasn't dealing with the reality that he had lost his eye," Rev. King said. "He was thinking he would be able to play again. I didn't do anything to discourage him. I wanted to bring him out of his grief."

There is no visible scarring around his left eye. The color of the artificial eye matches his real one.

Ronald Sims wears his dark brown sunglasses most of the time.

Compensation, but no career

He receives worker's compensation, $1,479 a month. For the next 10 years he will continue to receive part or all of it, the amount depending on how much he earns elsewhere. For the time being, he is earning nothing else.

A typical day, he said, starts with a check of the classified ads, a few phone calls, maybe a visit to a prospective employer. "I'm trying to find a job," he said. "Something, anything, just to have something to do."

The rest of the day, "I usually just hang out, practice baseball."

And he watches baseball, the Braves on television, and says to himself, "I should be out there."

He said he is planning to pursue a general equivalency diploma.

The Braves made good on Aaron's offer to find a place for Sims. "We're looking at a young man who didn't finish school," Gilbreath, the Braves' assistant scouting director, said. "What's he going to do between now and the time he gets his schooling, if he ever does go back? He has no job. What happened was, here's a guy who devoted his whole life to baseball and all of a sudden he can't play."

In March, the Braves employed Sims as a clubhouse manager at their minor-league complex in West Palm Beach, handling equipment and uniforms, coordinating clubhouse cleanup. He earned $800 for two weeks.

When camp broke he was asked to continue working at the Braves' extended spring training. "They wanted me to go to Bradenton. I didn't want to go down there - too many memories down there. So I told them I was coming home. Maybe I can do it next year."

Sims said he feels sort of cheated because the Braves never gave him a second chance to show whether he could still play. "They at least could have given me a shot, a tryout, to prove it one way or the other," he said.

According to Michelson's Book of World Baseball Records (Adams Press, 1985), there have been seven one-eyed ballplayers who played in the major leagues. Some lost their vision while playing, others beforehand.

All of them - Hi Jasper, Bill Irwin, Claude Jonnard, Tom Sunkel, Bob Mabe, Jack Franklin and Whammy Douglas - were pitchers and none lasted long or had much success.

As for the Braves' decision not to offer Sims another contract, Gilbreath explained: "We discussed it at length and because of the nature of the injury, we'd have a hard time running it past our insurance people. But we want to keep him involved with baseball. He's a class person. His family is class people. He's the kind of person we'd like to have around our players. If he wants to stay in baseball, it's up to him how far he can go."

Still holding onto his fame

Ronald Sims is still practicing baseball, in workouts with his former teammates and with the guys in the neighborhood.

"The only way I can see him playing pro ball is if he's a DH," said Szymanski, his former coach. "He was out there with us and he was trying to catch ground balls and he looked kind of awkward. I don't question his ability to hit, but I doubt he can play the field with one eye."

Sims has batted against the Satsuma High pitching machine and has put a few baseballs over that leftfield fence. He has yet to face a live pitcher, to face the prospect of a high-inside fastball.

He is still something of a local celebrity. He has been asked to throw out the first ball at a couple of youth baseball games, has signed a few autographs, and fans still slap him on the back and ask how it's going. "Everybody knows him, the whole community," his mother said. "They love him. They just cherish him."

Sims, soft-spoken, reserved, almost shy, sat on the sofa, toyed absent-mindedly with one of his trophies and smiled self-consciously at his mother's remark.

"It kind of makes me feel good, to know somebody recognizes you," he said. "I'm holding onto that."

But fame, even in the best of circumstances, can be fleeting.

"He's not letting go," his mother said. "I tell him every day, 'Just put your mind on something else.' He'll say, 'All right.' But deep down inside I think his mind is still only on playing ball. …

"He's a hero now 'cause he played baseball, 'cause of the accident. Two years down the road, he'll be just nothin'. Just Ronald Sims."

(May 14, 1989)

⁓ Ronald Sims, married with four children, still lives in Saraland, Ala., about two blocks from his parents' home. He briefly helped coach baseball at nearby schools. He works at a chemical plant in nearby Mobile. Napoleon Robinson got as far as Triple-A in the International League but never made it to the majors. ⁓

Fifteen

Too late, Maris gets the record

There never really was an asterisk to begin with.

More to the point, there should never have been one.

Roger Maris, whose only flaws were that he wasn't Mickey Mantle and that he wasn't Babe Ruth, has been vindicated … 30 years after the fact and six years after it really would have meant anything.

In 1961, Maris hit 61 home runs. On Wednesday, baseball formally and finally acknowledged him as the unquestioned single-season major-league home-run king. Too bad he isn't around to enjoy it.

When he died in 1985, he was still chained to Ruth's ghost.

"I'm sure he'd like to have seen that asterisk removed when he was still alive," Maris' 32-year-old son, Roger Jr., said by phone Wednesday from the Maris family beer distributorship in Gainesville. "But it was never that big of a deal to him. He always felt he had the record. If he was around today, I think the only thing he would be is amazed that it took 30 years to make it official.

"Campaigning (to formalize the record) is something he never did, something he would have never done, and we (his family) didn't do it, either, because we knew he wouldn't want us to. The way he looked at it, if it was meant to be, if people felt strongly enough about it, it would eventually happen."

On Wednesday it happened. An eight-man committee on statistical accuracy, chaired by commissioner Fay Vincent, voted unanimously to formally eliminate Ruth's 60 home runs from the record books.

When Maris hit his 61, the American League had just expanded from eight to 10 teams and from 154 to 162 games.

He had come to New York only the year before, to play side-by-side with Mantle in the Yankee outfield. As the two of them conducted their home-run derby, Maris became the home-town villain. If anyone was going to break Ruth's record, it was supposed to be Mantle.

Mantle was the hero-in-residence. By then, most Yankee fans had forgotten how much they had hated him for replacing Joe DiMaggio in the outfield.

On July 17, 1961, with Maris three weeks ahead of the home-run pace Ruth had set in 1927, commissioner Ford Frick proclaimed that Maris would have to hit 61 in 154 games to claim the record.

Maris failed to meet Frick' artificial deadline. He hit No. 61 in the final game of the season. Mantle finished with 54.

Frick hadn't always been a baseball bigwig. During the 1920s and '30s, Ruth's heyday, he had been a sports writer covering the Yankees for the New York *Journal*. He and Ruth had been close friends.

That Ruth's 60 homers in 154 games also had come in an era before night games, coast-to-coast travel, relief specialists, intense media scrutiny and the breaking of baseball's color line didn't concern Frick. Babe Ruth was baseball, and Frick would brook no tarnishing of a legend.

He never actually ordered an asterisk. He just decided that baseball should keep two sets of books. In 1962, and every year since then, Maris' 162-game record and Ruth's 154-game record were listed with separate but equal prominence.

When Eric Dickerson broke O.J. Simpson's single-season rushing record in 1984, NFL commissioner Pete Rozelle didn't take pains to point out he needed two more games to do it. When Bobby Hull took 65 games in 1965-66 to break the 50-goal record Maurice Richard had set in 50 games more than 20 years earlier, NHL commissioner Clarence Campbell didn't rush to Richard's defense.

Finally, baseball has come to its senses and acknowledged that a record is a record.

Of course, in a classic case of throwing out the baby with the bath water, baseball chose to right one wrong and, at the same time, to wrong some rights. Along with Ruth's non-record, it expunged from its records 50 no-hitters because they weren't "games of nine innings or more that ended with no hits."

All those five-inning, rain-shortened no-hitters surely were expendable. Maybe even Harvey Haddix's phenomenal performance in 1959, when he pitched 12 perfect innings for Pittsburgh against Milwaukee, losing 1-0 in the 13th on an error, a sacrifice and a Joe Adcock double.

"Haddix may have pitched one of the great games in baseball history," commissioner Vincent explained, "but it just doesn't happen to be a no-hit game."

Even Haddix couldn't argue the point. "When you think about it," he told The Associated Press, "that would be correct."

But what must Andy Hawkins be thinking? Last year he pitched a no-hitter for the Yankees in Chicago but lost 4-0. Because he was on the visiting team, he never got to pitch the ninth inning. Sorry,

121

baseball decreed. No no-hitter. Blame Mother Nature. Hawkins' byte in Baseball's official memory bank has been erased.

Oh, well. Maybe in another 30 years baseball will get around to fixing this little problem.

Or perhaps it'll just add an asterisk.

(September 5, 1991)

Roger Maris' 1961 record stood until 1999, when Mark McGwire of the St. Louis Cardinals hit 70 and Sammy Sosa of the Chicago Cubs hit 66. Their totals and Barry Bonds' 73 for the San Francisco Giants in 2001 have been called into question due to allegations the three used performance-enhancing drugs.

Sixteen

Caught in his own steel curtain

CLEARWATER, Fla. - The waiting room is uncompromisingly bleak. Gray benches. Gray doors. Dull blue tiles halfway up the cinder-block walls. Fluorescent lighting under the dirty white ceiling. The other doors lead to similarly dreary administrative offices, to class-rooms, to the intake area where newcomers are screened, to the two-to-a-room living quarters.

No door opens without the assent of the uniformed guard in mas-ter control. The noises ricochet incessantly. A raucous buzz precedes every opening of a door. A metallic slam follows it. The muffled voices of adults and children echo through the dimly lit halls.

This is Glen Edwards' world, the Pinellas County Juvenile Deten-tion Center, a lifetime and a fortune away from the natural grass and artificial turf he patrolled for a dozen years.

He used to make close to six figures a year. He could have had just about anything he wanted, and he had most of it. A condo in San Di-ego. A Mercedes.

Now, at 43, he makes about $1,300 a month and lives from pay-check to paycheck. He said he owes the Internal Revenue Service more money than he can ever hope to earn.

One steel curtain has supplanted another.

He has gone from being a free safety in the National Football League to a detention care worker fending off youngsters with an attitude, boys who will take a swing at him just on general principles.

"Basically, I'm a jailer," he said. "Actually, we're more than that. We're counselors. We're their momma and daddy. We're everything to them.

"But this is a very stressful job. These kids get physical with you. You have no idea what goes on in their minds. I've knocked out guys 250 (pounds). Then you get these little kids telling you what they're going to do you."

Almost reflexively, he put his forearm in front of his face.

"They'll come at you. Comes a time when you have to handle a kid who's beyond control. You never do it one-on-one. You've got to cover your a--. People will believe anything kids say. Ninety-nine percent of the time it's a lie, but there's going to be an investigation. All they've got to do is make the allegation. Like being a time bomb in here."

He was seated in a spartan office in the detention center. On his left hand was a massive gold ring with two diamonds, a memento of Pittsburgh's Super Bowl X victory over Dallas. He also has the ring commemorating the triumph over the Vikings the previous year.

"You hear these stories, 'He's so bad off he's sold his Super Bowl rings,' or, 'The IRS took 'em away,'" Edwards said with indifference. "I don't care what people say. Let 'em say what they want. People are going to believe anything they want, anyway. People want to see you do bad. It's the nature of man."

In the era of Jack Lambert, Jack Ham, L.C. Greenwood and Mean Joe Greene, the headliners of the Pittsburgh defense that propelled the Steelers to successive Super Bowl victories, Edwards was a supporting member of the cast.

Two of his memorable plays were an interception of Roger Staubach's end-zone pass on the final play of Super Bowl X, preserving

Pittsburgh's 21-17 victory over Dallas, and what appeared to be a helmet-to-helmet collision in Super Bowl IX with Minnesota receiver John Gilliam as he caught the ball on Pittsburgh's five-yard line, jarring it loose. It was intercepted on the goal line with about a minute to play in the first half.

Now Edwards is on the receiving end. He has been hit hard. And often. And not just by someone else's kids.

His 21-year marriage has unraveled. His driver's license has been suspended.

A small house that Edwards bought in 1972 in south St. Petersburg as income property is now home to him, the oldest of his four children, 18-year-old Landrick, and a nephew. A tenant lives upstairs. Edwards has no phone at home. A former roommate ran up a $600 bill calling sleazy 900 numbers, then took off, Edwards said.

Landrick dropped out of Osceola High School in the 11th grade and has worked off and on at odd jobs since. "I experience working here, seeing these kids," Edwards said, "then I go home and see my own kid wanting to be the same way."

Edwards said he grew up with the parents of some of the kids who eat, sleep and go to school at the detention center, some of them there for four months at a clip. He has to deal with 9-year-olds incarcerated for breaking and entering, selling drugs, stealing cars.

"Most of them, they're just preparing themselves for going from small-time jails to big-time jails," Edwards said. "Right now some of them have big-time charges against them and the system is just slapping them on the wrist."

He leaned back and spread his palms upward. "I don't have the answers. Not for these kids. I don't know, maybe not for my own. He has to find out for himself."

Glen Edwards knew by the time he was 6, long before he became a star athlete at Gibbs High School in St. Petersburg, that pro football was his goal.

Because he was sick as a youngster, he repeated second grade. And a knee injury at Florida A&M caused him to be redshirted. "Maybe if one of those things hadn't happened, maybe I wouldn't have been signed by the Steelers," he said. "Maybe I wouldn't have even played pro football. You never know."

He went from FAMU to the Steelers as a free agent in 1971 and stayed with Pittsburgh through its rise to dominance. He never returned to FAMU to complete his degree in education.

"It's tough to get back into (college life)," he said. "Success changes you, the good times. In the off-season you want to just kick back and do nothing. You say to yourself, 'One day I'm going to have to give this up,' but at the time it doesn't matter."

In 1977, unhappy over the Steelers' unwillingness to improve on his contract, Edwards staged a one-man, one-week walkout during the season. The following season he was traded to San Diego. In 1981 he earned $97,000. He would have made $108,000 in 1982, he said, but the Chargers waived him, then re-signed him after the strike that season.

The next year he was out of the NFL for good. He spent the 1983 spring season with the USFL's Tampa Bay Bandits and, at 36, was finished.

A dozen years from now he'll begin collecting $1,635 a month in NFL retirement benefits.

"I tell guys now that there's three steps in football … they get you, they trade you and they get rid of you for good," Edwards said. "Until a guy experiences that third step, you never know what it's like.

"If your age doesn't get you, your salary will. They'll either tell you you're too old or not worth it. The bottom line is, it's a business. Nobody understands that unless you've experienced it as a player. Just like winning the Super Bowl. You have to experience it to understand it."

When the Steelers began winning Super Bowls, Edwards and some teammates got involved in questionable investments, tax shelters like coal mines. Early on, he'd put in $12,000 and get back $20,000. That lasted a year, he said. After that, he'd pump in more money and never see it.

And there was the matter of the taxes. California said he owed $30,000. He paid that off in one lump sum. The federal government said he owed about $22,000. He's been trying to pay that off for years. With interest and penalties, the bill is up to about $45,000, Edwards said. He said the IRS seized the Mercedes and has put a lien on his house.

"They could take it all, take everything, and I couldn't pay it off in 10 lifetimes," he said.

Two Super Bowl rings and a dozen years in pro football's defensive backfields don't open many doors. He said he didn't have the money to return to FAMU. "Even if I went back, who knows whether it would have made a big difference?"

When his playing days ended, Edwards tried landscaping. But it takes money to pay workers, to buy equipment. The business failed.

He got three jobs ... the one at the detention center, one at an employment office, and one loading and unloading cruise ships. "But the employment office job was just temporary," he said, "and then the cruise ships stopped coming to St. Petersburg."

It haunts him, Edwards said, that there was a time in his life when he could have anything he wanted, that his children never wanted for anything. He says Landrick remembers what it was like 10 years ago and it hurts that he can't give him now what he could give him then.

"One day, all this stuff's going to turn around," Edwards said. "I read the Bible every once in a while. I know this is a test, that everything happens for a reason. I ain't done nothin' wrong."

(August 8, 1990)

~ *Glen Edwards later worked in construction before retiring in 2007. His Super Bowl rings are gone. He said he gave one to a drug dealer in exchange for a $20 loan he never repaid and said the other vanished after he asked a friend to keep it while he was trying to recover from an addiction.* ~

Seventeen

Hungry heart

ATLANTA - That rumble you hear coming out of the South Pacific is not some tsunami consuming everything in its path. It is the hunger pangs of an entire nation.

It is fasting today for Paea Wolfgramm.

Tonga, that assemblage of 170 volcanic and coral islands in the Greater Western Samoa/Fiji metropolitan area, has its first Olympic medal, compliments of Wolfgramm, a super-heavyweight boxer who probably has been mistaken more than once for the 171st island.

"Man steps into the ring, he blocks out the light," U.S. boxing coach Al Mitchell said. "Throws those big fists from all over the place. He's got a roundhouse left could knock down a buffalo. Do they have buffalo in Tonga? Whatever, he's got power, no doubt about that. And He's got confidence. One thing he doesn't lack, confidence."

Paea (PAY-uh) Wolfgramm was named Tonga's Best Boxer in 1995 and '96. Part of the reason, he suggested, is because "boxing in Tonga consists of one boxer ... me."

Tonga's only other boxer to leave an imprint on the Olympics was Tevita Toufou. He won one bout in 1984, his country's Olympics debut.

'We pray and know'

Wolfgramm is huge back in Tonga, 309 pounds' worth.

Well, maybe he's not all that huge, relatively speaking. First of all, he's down from the 350 he weighed a year ago.

And the king of Tonga, Taufa'hau Tupou IV, is no tadpole. He weighs in at an even 300.

Nevertheless, Wolfgramm is the biggest thing to hit Tonga since Capt. James Cook stumbled upon it 223 years ago.

Wolfgramm also is the biggest thing ever to hit Alexis Rubalcaba, the Cuban super-heavyweight who had been an overwhelming favorite to win the Olympic gold medal.

In Tonga, all day Tuesday before Wolfgramm's quarterfinal match, most if not all of the population of 106,000 fasted through three meals for him. "They put out the word that I was fighting," he said. "They were fasting the day before. ... It's a very religious country."

Then Wolfgramm went out Wednesday night and dropped Rubalcaba on the seat of his trunks before most of the patrons at Georgia Tech's Alexander Memorial Coliseum had a chance to wonder whether Wolfgramm had a chance.

Two standing 8-counts and three rounds later, Wolfgramm was a decisive winner.

Tony Fulilangi, his friend and coach, explained that the heavily Mormon population is a God-loving, faithful people, "and so if we pray and fast for something, we do so knowing that it is given to us....

"We don't pray and wait," Fulilangi said. "We pray and know. We pray and believe we're going to win. This victory was given to Paea."

Wolfgramm never had fought anyone beyond the Pacific. That alone made the victory a major accomplishment. More to the point, he had beaten a Cuban. Beating a Cuban in the ring is like beating Johnnie Cochran in a courtroom. Wolfgramm said that as far as he was concerned, he already had won his gold medal.

In fact, it assured him of a bronze.

And that, too, was good enough - for Tonga. Wolfgramm said King Tupou sent him a telegram telling him: "Anything else is a bonus; you've done really well."

Well, not well enough for Wolfgramm.

Thursday, Tonga went hungry again.

Wolfgramm was boxing again.

This time the tightness in Tongan stomachs was more than the absence of comestibles. Wolfgramm had to rally from a two-point deficit in the final round Friday night against Nigeria's Duncan Dokiwari, and his decisive punch came 15 seconds from the final bell.

So the 21,383 good people of the Tonganese capital of Taufa'ahau and the rest of Wolfgramm's countrymen will awaken today with Georgia in their hearts and food on their minds, food they will not have touched all day Saturday, food they may not touch until today's gold-medal bout with Vladimir Klichko of Ukraine ends.

If Wolfgramm's hand is raised in triumph, all of Tonga will feast on his victory. If it is not, well, more than a few people have been known to drown their sorrows in calories.

Guts and enthusiasm

One thing is certain. Klichko might as well call himself Vlad the Bad. He might as well enter the ring wearing a cape or a mask, or clubbing a baby seal. He may help little old ladies across the street back home, he may conduct bake sales, he may support his local police. But here he is the heavy in more than weight.

He is about to find himself awash in Paeamania.

The spectators at the boxing venue have taken the massive Wolfgramm to their hearts, chanting "Ton-ga! Ton-ga!'" at every opportunity. When you have almost nobody local to root for - and the United States has pretty much taken care of that, light middleweight David Reid being the remaining American - you latch on to someone else who strikes your fancy.

"And Wolfgramm has been striking everyone's fancy.

"The whole of Tonga has been uplifted," Fred Sevele, secretary general of Tonga's Olympic Committee, told Reuters. "This is going to do a lot of good to our sports. At the moment we don't have the facilities, we don't have the financial resources. But we have got the guts and enthusiasm. For a population of 100,000 it's not too bad."

'I spar with anybody'

Wolfgramm was born Tongan and moved with his parents and four older siblings to New Zealand, three hours away by air, when he was 5. He has however, maintained strong ties with his homeland, visiting often. He is fluent in Tongan and English. Rugby, no delicate game, was his early sport of choice. When he sustained an injury in a match, he began boxing as a form of rehabilitation.

He started hitting people seriously in 1990 when Fulilangi - who the year before had gone less than two rounds against another behemoth, George Foreman - got a good look at his technique, saw potential and persuaded Wolfgramm to drop out of the University of Auckland to give boxing a serious shot.

Soon he was having trouble finding sparring partners. "Basically, I spar with anybody that gets in the ring with me," he said.

Like most of his countrymen, he is a devout Mormon. He and his wife, Vanessa, an airline clerk, have three sons, and she supports him. He still likes rugby and likes still life. He sketches.

Wolfgramm does have a job - "I'm a mild-mannered clerk" with a telecommunications firm in Auckland - but on his Olympic biography he listed his principal occupation as "house husband."

If he beats Klichko - or even if he doesn't - Wolfgramm will have a new job the next time he sets foot in his homeland:

Hero.

"I think the king will want to give me half the island or something," he said.

(August 4, 1996)

∼ Paea Wolfgramm, fighting with a broken nose and broken wrist, lost to Klichko on points. His silver was Tonga's first Olympic medal. On March 18, 2000, Klichko stopped Wolfgramm in the first round to win the vacant WBC title. Wolfgramm retired in 2001 attempted a comeback two years later but lost by a decision his final bout. ∼

Eighteen

Rebel has a cause

ST. PETERSBURG - Dock Ellis reached for the sugar and emptied a handful of packets into his coffee.

"When I was at The Meadows, I was a peer leader," he said. "He's the guy who'd go into town, buy toiletries or whatever the group needed. One old guy, he told me, 'Bring me back 12 candy bars - six Hershey's with almonds, six without.' I told him, 'Man, are you crazy? You're gonna die!' He told me, 'Don't worry, kid. Just wait'll you get out of here.'"

The Meadows is an alcohol-and-drug-rehabilitation facility in Wickenburg, Ariz. It was October 1980 and Ellis, less than a year removed from his 12th and final season as a major-league pitcher, was undergoing 45 days of treatment.

"When I got out, I found myself eating six Snickers a day. I told my mother and she said, 'You used to eat Paydays like that when you were a little boy.' I called my counselor and told him, 'This candy's gonna blow me up. What's goin' on?' And he told me my body was craving sugar. There's a whole bunch of sugar in alcohol.

"He told me to try and cut back to one candy bar at breakfast, another at lunch, another at dinner, like a diet. Then I noticed the attacks, two or three a year. I see sugar, I want it. I don't usually drink coffee. Coffee goes with sugar."

The waitress served breakfast. Ellis grabbed the syrup and drowned his pancakes in it.

"Once you get sugar he said, "you want more sugar."

Once an addict, always an addict.

Dock Ellis, 44, is the pitching coach and occasional relief pitcher for the St. Petersburg Pelicans. He wasn't drafted when the Senior Professional Baseball Association was formed. But he grew up with Bobby Tolan, now the Pelicans manager, so he called his boyhood friend and got a tryout.

Ellis also is an alcoholic, a former drug abuser, a man with an addictive personality. You name it, he has ingested it - booze before he was 4, marijuana as a teen-ager, then Benzedrine and Dexamil and other amphetamines, and LSD and cocaine and even a little heroin.

When he pitched for Pittsburgh during 1968-75, and when he bounced from the Yankees to Oakland to Texas to the Mets and back to the Pirates in the next four seasons, Dock Ellis was considered one of baseball's pre-eminent weirdos.

He pitched a no-hitter against the Padres in 1970 while under the influence of drugs. "I went to a Cocaine Anonymous meeting the other day," he said shortly after the start of the SPBA season. "I was scared to death. I had never pitched and not been high. Never."

He wore hair curlers during the summer of '73. "I couldn't throw spitballs with K-Y Jelly or Vaseline or slippery elm. I couldn't control the ball. With the perm, my head sweated from the chemicals. If I touched the back of my hair, it was like putting my hand in a bucket of water."

He was routinely outrageous.

"Oh, yeah," he said, "Now they call it outspoken. It used to be that if you were outspoken, you were a flake. Unless you were black. Then you were militant.

"I was known as individual who didn't bull---- but I was not a 'team player' 'cause I'd talk my piece. I won't bull---- when it comes to drugs and alcohol. I had a lot of animosity toward baseball. Now I've changed. I can help."

He has gone through three marriages. He has a 20-year-old daughter in California from the first one, a 10-year-old son in Texas from the second, and a 3-year-old daughter in New Jersey from the third.

"I was a drunk before I had a drink," he said. "I was destined to be a drunk. It was in my genes."

He said his grandfather was an alcoholic, that his godfather used to drink boilermakers - beer with vodka chasers - and that at the age of 3, "I drank what I saw. I thought it was water. I'd see that glass (of vodka) and drink that 'water.' They'd be looking for me and I'd be out in the corner, asleep."

He resumed drinking when he was 11 or 12 to be one of the guys, he said, then moved up to more serious stuff. "I was heavily into cocaine in the early '70s," and he experimented with heroin, snorting it.

Once, in Los Angeles, he came close to mainlining. "I called a friend, asked him for $500 in heroin and a kit (a spoon to cook it and a needle to inject it). He came to my room, brought this guy to show me how to do it. I told him, 'I don't need nobody to show me. I got a junkie with me. A lady.'"

But he changed his mind, Ellis said, and "flushed it down the toilet. The lady cried for three hours."

He would do it all again. "If my life didn't go this way," he said, "I wouldn't be the person I am today. I don't regret nothin' I did. If I had to do it over, I'd do it the same damn way."

Even the alcohol, the drugs, the pain?

"I loved it," Ellis said. His eyes were wide now, the excitement, the passion dancing in them. "You don't understand what it's like.

"I loved it. I loved the feeling. The more I had, the more I wanted to do.

"I loved it. Some alcoholics say they didn't like the taste. I loved the taste of alcohol.

"I loved it. I loved the drip of cocaine down my nose. I loved it.

"I loved the way it tasted. I loved the way it made me feel. I loved the way it made me have dry mouth.

""I loved it. I loved to wake up in the morning and be dry-heaving over the toilet bowl, just hugging the bowl. I loved to be on the cold floor, naked. I loved the feeling.

"I loved it. I loved the feeling of being high. I loved the shakes. I knew if I did a lot of cocaine and Courvoisier that the next morning I could squat down like I never squatted before and hug that toilet bowl and yellow s--- come out of my mouth. And lay down on the cold floor, get buck-naked, and feel that cold. I loved that."

There is a saying that there is no one more reformed than a re-formed drunk. Ellis is the definitive reformer.

When his baseball career ended, he wasn't traveling as much, and the drugs weren't as plentiful. He began relying more and more on alcohol once again, mostly Scotch. He hated Scotch. "What got me to treatment," he said, "was that old saying we have in the program, that I got sick and tired of being sick and tired."

He called Don Newcombe, the former Brooklyn Dodgers pitcher, a recovered alcoholic who has helped other addicts. Newk got Dock into The Meadows.

"They educated me, made me understand what was wrong with me, why I was sick like that," Ellis said. "I had a disease. You can't scare anyone who's on drugs. You have to educate them."

Ellis swears he has never relapsed, and that it's not as unusual as some might think.

"There's a lot of us," he said. "That's something else I don't like (about most treatment programs). They teach the kids, 'You're gonna slip.' That's bull----. If I was in treatment and somebody were to tell me, 'Well, you're gonna slip one time, so don't worry about it,' that's the first thing I'd do when I got out. I'd get high. 'Oh, I slipped.'"

Once clean, Ellis said, he took psychology and counseling courses, then began working with alcoholics and drug-abusers. He was the Yankees' substance-abuse counselor for their minor-league system the past three years.

Beer is one of sports' principal sponsors, even a principal owner of some franchises. Former athletes sell their names to sell beer. "There's greed all the way around," Ellis said. "You've got to convince (owners and players) to give up those commercial dollars.

"Baseball is never going to admit it has a drug problem. All that stuff they say about how they want to clean up their act, they're just reading from a script. And the players association hasn't done a damned thing about it."

He thinks America's war against drugs should start with the shooting down of planes even suspected of smuggling heroin and cocaine into the United States, and thorough examinations of everyone and everything coming into the country.

He thinks baseball's war against drugs and alcohol should start with the players' first day in the minors. The players association is currently limited to major-league membership and has no say in minor-league operations.

"Management has to educate players," Ellis said. "And the union's got to tell the players, 'You have X amount of time to clean yourself up or you're out. This is the way it's going to be.' The players association has got to clamp down," to be willing to accept - to insist on - periodic testing from the first day a player turns pro, so that by the time he gets to the majors he will be educated and testing will be a fact of life.

"And you know what else will happen? Families will be helped," Ellis said. "A lot of wives go through hell, and they're sickos, too, 'cause they stick with those stupid sons-of-b------ because they want those big cars and credit cards.

Education is the only way, he said, expanding his argument from baseball to society in general.

"There's always going to be alcoholics and drugs addicts, because some people are destined to be that way. But if you can teach kids A-B-C, you can teach them about drugs and alcohol. Start in kindergarten. Before.

"Kids have little, bitty eyes. They watch you, emulate mommy and daddy. If parents do drugs, they're going to do the same damn thing. They see and hear everything. When they get to kindergarten, they already know a lot. You've got to tell them, 'What's this? What's that?' Got to let them smell this and smell that. It's going to take two or three generations, but we've got to do it."

(November 14, 1989)

～ Dock Ellis died December 19, 2008, at the Los Angeles County-USC Medical Center of cirrhosis of the liver. He was 63. ～

Nineteen

The life and times of Pistol Pete

CLEARWATER - The boy is going to have to be able to dribble a bas-ketball while riding a bicycle, to dribble while hanging out the window of a car, to blind-pass the ball behind his back, between his legs ...

That's the way Pete Maravich did it.

It's been eight years since he played in the NBA, eight months since he lost his father, Press, to cancer.

It's been 37 years since Press handed his 3-year-old son a basket-ball and said, "Play!"

Few did it with the commitment of Pistol Pete.

His father would never let him shoot the ball. Bounce it, yes. Throw it, yes. But shoot it, never.

"Can I take a shot?"

"No, you're too little. Go back in the house."

He was baiting his son. He didn't want the boy to feel about basketball the way he would feel about football or baseball. He wanted it to be so special that it would push everything else out of the boy's life.

The boy got discouraged. He told his mother he didn't want to play with the basketball anymore.

"Why don't you ask your father if he'll let you shoot?"

"He won't let me."

"If he doesn't let you play today, you can take up something else and forget about him."

The boy went out and peeked around the corner of the house. His father saw him.

"Come here, Pete!"

The boy went over and asked if he could take a shot.

"Yes - one - if you let me teach you how to hold the ball and how to shoot."

They spent 10 minutes on fundamentals. The shot didn't come close to the basket. The rim was 10 feet high, regulation height.

The boy ran into the house. "Mom! He let me shoot. He let me play with him!"

Of course, it had been a set-up. It had worked. Pete Maravich was hooked on basketball.

Nutrition and religion

He does two or three speaking engagements a month, weaving together his basketball and born-again Christianity. He is, he says, a 24-hour traveler, flying to his game or speaking engagement, then flying right back home to Covington, La., to Jackie and their sons, Jaeson, 8, and Joshua, 5.

Maravich cleared out his condominium on Clearwater Beach last week. It's been sold. He hadn't lived there much the past few years, anyway, preferring Covington and family to Sand Key and seagulls.

He'll be back in June to run Pistol Pete's Basketball Camp at Clearwater Christian College. He started it in 1983, dedicating it to the work ethic, with a liberal dose of nutrition and religion, and now has similar camps in North Carolina and Texas. He talks about franchising them "if I can find the right kind of people to run them."

Maravich does TV color commentary at college games, some on the USA network, some for NBC, some on Louisiana State's regional network.

Press coached at LSU and Pete played there. Eighteen seasons later, he still holds most of the school basketball records.

He has made the Homework basketball series, instructional videos "based on something my dad developed 30 years ago. You don't really have to have a gym except for the shooting. The other parts are passing, dribbling and ball-handling and spinning. Those you can do at home."

He is promoting the series, and is pushing his book, *Heir to a Dream*, published last month. It is about his relationship with his father and with his mother, who took her life 13 years ago.

And he is talking about a movie.

Hooked again

Press came in one day - Pete was 8 then - and snapped, "I don't understand it. That boy just doesn't have it, Helen. He'll never make it. He just quits."

The woman looked at her husband and said, "Why don't you let him win once?" The boy would play his father one-on-one and, no matter how he tried, he couldn't come close to winning.

This afternoon, the boy was in his room, crying.

His father came in. "Hey," he told his son, "let's go. I want to play you one more time today."

"I don't want to play you anymore."

"C'mon, just one more."

"No!"

Finally the boy relented. He beat his father by one point. The father made it look as though he'd really tried.

The boy ran into the house. "Mom! I beat dad! I beat dad!"

He was hooked again.

'My boy can do that'

The movie is to be about a year in the life of Pistol Pete, when he was a 5-foot-2, 90-pound 13-year-old in Clemson, S.C., practicing 10 hours a day, dribbling the ball to and from school, in school, in his room, his back yard - everywhere but in church.

A few weeks ago they tried to cast the starring role. They advertised the audition in Baton Rouge. More than 300 kids showed up. A wire service picked up the story. That's when the phone calls started.

"Every day it was, 'Hey, my boy can do that.' " It has become a series of tryouts across the nation. The movie, if it is made at all, will be released in January 1989, in the middle of the basketball season.

Practicing the Pretzel

Press was watching Gunsmoke, watching two men standing in the street, waiting for each other to draw. From that, he thought up a basketball drill.

"C'mere," the father said to his 13-year-old son. "Stand up straight. Hands down at your sides. I'm going to put this basketball between your shoulder blades. I'm going to drop it - I'm not going to tell you when - and when I do I want you to clap your hands in front of you and then catch the ball in back."

It was weeks before his son could do it. After a while, it was just another exercise in boredom. The son rebelled. He didn't want to have anything to do with his father's drills.

The boy adored one of the assistant coaches at Clemson. One day the assistant came by. "Hey Pete, I just had this idea." He held the ball between his legs with his hands, one hand behind his left knee, the other in front of his right knee. "Then you try and change hands as fast as you can as often as you can so the ball doesn't hit the floor. Try it."

"Wow! That's great!'

He spent weeks practicing the Pretzel, and later some other drills.

He never realized it was his father's doing.

'Did you hear Him?'

"My dad was always my hero," he said. "I didn't have a rock-star hero, an athlete hero. I think that's good, that we should want to please our fathers, that they should be our heroes. We shouldn't have to look outward from our own family."

These days, Pete Maravich spends most of his time practicing his religion. He is well off, he says, but his days of conspicuous consumption are over.

"We fill our lives with things. Get, get, get. Reach the top rung. At 7 I had goals. One day I would have all the money I needed, I'd be able to play the game, then retire, go home, dangle a toe in the swimming pool.

"I was left totally empty by it all. I couldn't have put another thing in my life that would have given me satisfaction. I'd reached the top rung. I'd reached my goals and I was terribly despondent."

He dabbled in the occult - reincarnation, yoga, transcendental meditation, astral-projection. In November of 1982, he was living in Metarie, La., in a $350,000 house with a BMW, a Mercedes-Benz and a Porsche in the driveway. He could do anything he wanted to do, go anywhere he wanted to. He was loved by family, by friends.

He was miserable.

He lay in bed, wide awake and troubled. It was 5:20 in the morning. With Jackie asleep beside him, he cried out silently, "Oh, God, can you forgive me?"

He says he heard God. "Right in that room he spoke to me, audibly. He said, 'Be true and lift thine own heart.' " He shook Jackie awake.

"Did you hear Him?'

"Who?" His wife figured this was just the latest aberration, that it, too, would pass.

'Who's Pistol Pete?'

Pete Maravich at 40 looks pale, gaunt, tired, except for the eyes. The fire burns brightly there.

"Choices," he was saying animatedly. "We all have choices. You either believe in the Bible or you don't."

He was wound up, not quite proselytizing - but close, speaking rapid-fire, punching the air.

"Jesus Christ said, 'I am the way, the truth and the light. No one comes to the Father but through Me.' Now either he is the truth, or he isn't. I'm not trying to make you a Christian. That's your choice. But I found the truth. I know where I'm going."

He is heading home to Covington. His sons will be in his camp this summer. They will play basketball.

Jaeson didn't start playing until he was 6, until he'd seen one of Pete's NBA highlight videotapes.

"Hey, Jaeson, come look at this basketball film."

"I don't want to."

"Okay, but I'll put it on anyway. Maybe Josh wants to watch it."

It was Pete baiting the hook.

"Jaeson must have watched that video 75 times in the next month and a half," Maravich said. "Until then, he never really knew who I was. There was nothing in my house to suggest it. All the trophies went in attics, places like that. In the first grade, he came home one day and told me, 'Some kid says you're Pistol Pete. Who's Pistol Pete?' That's when I sat him down, told him who I was, what I'd done.

"After he'd watched that film, he got an insatiable urge to play. I wanted to teach him how to play. He didn't want me to. I told him, 'If you're going to learn how to play, you're going to do it right.' I spent an hour or two teaching him, then I left him alone."

Jaeson Maravich plays every day now. But not 10 hours a day, his father said. "He doesn't have to be Pistol Pete."

(December 24, 1987)

In a 1974 interview with the Beaver County (Pa.) Times, Pete Maravich was quoted as saying: "I don't want to play 10 years in the NBA and die of a heart attack at age 40." He played in the NBA for 10 seasons. On January 5, 1988, just 12 days after the publication of this story, Maravich collapsed during a pickup game at a church gym in Pasadena, Calif., and died of an undiagnosed congenital heart defect. He was 40. A movie, Pistol: Birth of a Legend, was released in 1991.

Twenty

Pain of the gain

The flight to Brazil aboard the Varig airliner took close to 12 hours. The ventilation was next to nonexistent. The flight attendants spoke Portuguese. And Leila Pallardy was sick as a dog.

She spent most of the flight throwing up. With hand signals and visual aids (airsick bags and towels), the stewardesses told Jean Pallardy to clean up after her 12-year-old daughter.

By the time the plane landed in Sao Paulo, site of the Pan American Games, Leila Pallardy was physically and emotionally exhausted.

As the 4-foot-7, 78-pound gymnast from Tampa, a member of the U.S. junior team, lay across a luggage rack, her mother approached the U.S. judge for the tournament. Jean Pallardy knew … and U.S. gymnastics coach Kevin Brown had told her … that judges are skittish about parents accompanying their children to competitions (they often don't stay at the same hotel when they do come along). But her daughter barely could walk. This was an extraordinary circumstance.

"I asked the judge: 'Would you please let Leila rest and eat some crackers and drink some juice when she gets to the hotel?' I wanted to get some sodium, some potassium, some liquid into her.

"The judge looked at me and said: 'What kind of crackers?' I told her I'd packed some Ritz crackers. She said: 'She can't eat Ritz crackers. They have butter in them!'"

It was Dec. 7, 1992, and it was Jean Pallardy's moment of reckoning. Her daughter had been an elite gymnast with Olympic potential for a year and a half, "and there'd been these, y'know, hints along the way. That was when I decided for sure: 'There are people in this business who are crazy.'"

There is an ironic epilogue of sorts to this snapshot in time. "After the competition," Jean Pallardy recalled, "that same judge pointed out Leila and asked Kevin Brown: 'Does she have an eating disorder? She's so thin.'"

Few moments in the Summer Olympics are as breathtaking as watching a female gymnast do back handsprings and layouts on the balance beam, or double-layout backflips in the floor exercises … porcelain ballerinas defying gravity.

Boxers, swimmers, divers, sprinters, they may be our quadrennial heroes. But the little girls in tights and ponytails, they are our darlings.

From Nadia Comaneci to Mary Lou Retton, we adore such immense talent packed into such tiny frames. We look at our own daughters and wonder: What if we'd taken them to the gym more often? What if they'd stuck with the leaping and tumbling they so enjoyed at all those preschool birthday parties?

Some do … hundreds of thousands of them, perhaps millions. Right after the Olympic medals are handed out to these nimble figurines, parents begin stuffing their daughters into leotards and sending them off to the nearest floor mats, the little girls (and their parents) dreaming of a gaudy ribbon and a hunk of gold on the world's biggest stage.

"It's very common for parents and kids to set their sights too high," said Jeff LaFleur, a coach for more than 20 years with gyms in Tampa,

St. Petersburg and Largo. "It's good for kids to idolize, to be able to dream. Every kid who comes into the gym fantasizes about a gold medal in the Olympics, just as every Little Leaguer who watches Ken Griffey Jr. says to himself: 'That's going to be me.'

"Where it gets unrealistic is in the trenches (when serious competition begins). Then it's usually the parents," LaFleur said. "I usually have to tell them to chill. Don't drive them so hard. Don't try to live through them. I've seen parents take medals off their kids at meets and put 'em on themselves."

Melanie Robinson, 15, of Brandon is a Level 10 gymnast ... one step below elite but a big step, sort of like comparing college football to the NFL. Whether Melanie could have made elite does not matter here. What matters, she said, is that she saw what it could have done to her.

"I didn't want to be a burnout," Robinson said. "Two years ago (when she reached level 10), I put the brakes on. Seeing the training they had to do, that was too much." She wants a gymnastics scholarship to pave her road to college.

'Have her here next Monday'

Leila Pallardy began gymnastics at the age of 5, training at LaFleur's gym in Tampa. She was 9 when she spent two summer weeks in Houston at the camp run by Bela Karolyi, who had made Nadia Comaneci and Mary Lou Retton gold medalists.

"He called us," Jean Pallardy said, "and said he wanted her for his Olympic Hopes team (youngsters who produce the next wave of potential medalists ... and keep the pressure on the current, older ones). 'Have her here next Monday.' If she was going to be a champion, he said, she had to be there."

Jean Pallardy told her daughter about the phone call. It was an honor, she told Leila, just to be asked. What did she want to do?

Leila burst into tears. She didn't want to leave home.

"I said to myself: 'Thank you, Lord,'" Jean recalled. "I was concerned that she'd want to go. We didn't want her to go. Then we'd have had to deal with the 'You didn't let me go; you held me back' business."

The phone call still chills her. "I had to really rein in my emotions. He was so casual about it - 'Have her here next Monday.' I thought: 'You're talking about my firstborn and you're making it sound like I'm shipping out a package, like she's some kind of product.' I couldn't believe it."

Consumed by the sport

All but the smallest minority of gymnasts eventually come to treat the sport as a byproduct of youth, to be outgrown and abandoned. Of that remaining minority, some girls … and more often than not one or both parents … become consumed by the sport, driven to pile perfection upon perfection, to create an elite gymnast, a member of the national team, perhaps even an Olympian.

Some families split up to pursue the dream, one parent moving with the gymnast to a coach's city while the rest of the family remains home. Sometimes the split ends in divorce. Some parents ship their daughter to the coach, all but abrogating their responsibilities as mothers and fathers.

At what cost?

There are fewer than 200 elite female gymnasts in the United States, including 20 on the national team and just six who will compete at Atlanta in the 1996 Summer Olympics.

To become this best of the best, some of the girls will starve themselves. They may become anorexic or bulimic. Some of the girls' bodies will be ravaged by injuries, many of which will go untreated because even the briefest interruption in training is frowned upon by the sport's premier coaches.

"A lot of times they suffer broken bones and don't even know it, because they get so accustomed to the pain on a daily basis," said Kathy Johnson of Altamonte Springs, whose daughter Brandy was a 1988 Olympian. "There were times Brandy was hurting and she didn't want to know how bad it was for fear that it was going to keep her from doing what she wanted to do."

The pounding and poor diet can delay the onset of puberty, of menstruation, perhaps for years. That, in turn, can wreak havoc with bone structure … which can cause still more severe and longer-lasting injuries.

'A survivor of the system'

The psychological trauma may be equally devastating. When a girl's entire being is wrapped up in gymnastics, in pleasing her coach, and that overbearing coach drives her mercilessly, demanding greater and greater perfection, the results can be fatal. Girls who have failed to live up to sometimes impossible standards (a coach's, a judge's or their own) have attempted suicide.

Christy Henrich … who began her gymnastics career at the age of 4, was 4 feet 11 and 93 pounds at the peak of her career, and barely missed making the 1988 U.S. Olympic team … died 15 months ago after a long battle with eating disorders. She was 22. She weighed 50 pounds.

"A lot of them, the kids who don't quite make it, they think of themselves as total failures," said the now-married Brandy Johnson-Scharpf. "They don't know how to do anything but gymnastics."

For the very few American female gymnasts who do achieve their ultimate goal there is the potential for endorsement and appearance fees, for a television or movie career.

Retton, gold medalist at the 1984 Los Angeles Olympics, converted her instant of success to commercial cash. Cathy Rigby did the same almost solely on the strength of her personality and a silver medal at the 1970 world championships (she failed to medal in the '68 or '72 Olympics).

For others who reach that elite level, there will be varying degrees of success. They may become nationally known, even if they fail to win a world championship or an Olympic medal. Some may stay with the sport as professionals on tour, as coaches, instructors or broadcasters. Some may leave it with rich, fond memories of going places and doing things that most teenagers can barely imagine.

"If I had it to do over again, I'd do it all, no question," Johnson-Scharpf said. "I still love the sport (she performs professionally). It's something I hope will always be a part of me."

In a sense, it certainly will be. At 22, she has foot and ankle problems, bone chips, bursitis and arthritis, and likely will for the rest of her life. She says she is overcoming an eating disorder. "I can't eat in front of other people unless I'm real close with them. If I'm at some sort of celebrity dinner, it doesn't matter what the food is, I'll find a way to not eat it. Sign autographs. Talk to people. Anything."

Is gymnastics worth all those physical and psychological problems? "To me, absolutely," Johnson-Scharpf said.

Still, Kathy Johnson calls her daughter "a survivor of the system." And Brandy calls herself "one of the lucky ones."

'I didn't lose anything'

To Leila Pallardy, gymnastics was more job than joy. She had been Florida's vault champion at Level 4; uneven-bars champion at Level 6; regional all-around champion at Level 8; eastern all-around champion at Level 9; all-around champion in her first elite meet, the 1992 American Classic; all-around champion at the International Junior Invitational; a member of the silver-medal team at the 1992 Pan American Games…

And she wanted out. "The hardest decision was to actually quit," she said, "because gymnastics was all I knew. That was my life." Her only close friends were gymnasts. Schoolmates had long since stopped calling her, knowing she'd never have time for them.

"The feeling kind of crept up on me," she said. "I never thought I could do it. I was going to try for the Olympics and be the next Mary Lou."

But with age comes wisdom. There came a time when Leila Pallardy, a 4-foot-8, 70-pound seventh-grader, began thinking about the tricks she had done earlier without thinking. "I began to realize what I was actually doing, that I could kill myself."

For three months, she wrestled alone with her quandary. She was afraid to tell her parents. "They'd never pushed me," she said, "but they'd put so much money and time and energy into my life. I felt I had to give something back."

One evening, back home from Brazil, she and her mother sat in the living room, watching a TV movie. Tears began spilling down her cheeks.

"Mom," she said, "I don't want to do gymnastics anymore."

Jean looked at her daughter. "I know," she said.

The weight, so to speak, was off Leila's back. In the year and a half after she quit, she grew about 9 inches and gained 50 pounds.

She is a sophomore at Plant High School now, a cheerleader and member of the track team. She has begun dabbling with gymnastics again at the Interbay YMCA, just for fun. She wants to attend Notre Dame, which doesn't have a gymnastics program.

Would Leila Pallardy do it all again? Yes. Would she take it as seriously as she did. Yes. She was a member of the national team. She got to go places and do things that few teenagers can imagine. And now she's an average teenager. "I didn't lose anything," she said. "I just caught up to it later."

(October 15, 1995)

～ Leila Pallardy Shea has left gymnastics behind. After graduating from the University of Florida and earning a Master's degree she taught elementary school for seven years. She also coached gymnastics during and after college. She says she will enroll her two children in gymnastics at the appropriate time but won't push them or prevent them from continuing it. Leila Pallardy Shea can no longer participate – it left her with bad knees and a bad disc in her neck - but says, "I quit in time to catch up with my growth." ～

Twenty-one

Evel Irony

CLEARWATER - The Last of the Gladiators leans forward, starts to get up, sinks back wearily into the couch, and says, "Hand me my cane, will you?"

In our imagination, Evel Knievel still stands on the footpegs of his motorcycle and flies to the clouds and back, cheating death and laughing in its face. He is 59 now. Sixty will be a gift.

All the times he could have been killed - soaring over cars and buses and the fountains at Caesars Palace - and a total hip replacement and pelvic reconstruction in December after a fall on a golf course temporarily slows him to a trudge.

All the booze he consumed (half a fifth of Wild Turkey a day, with beer chasers, he says), all the women he slept with (usually one or two a day, some with very jealous husbands, he says), and hepatitis C from a tainted blood transfusion threatens to kill him.

Eighteen years ago he gave up trying to be what we expected of him, because we always expected more. He wasn't going to kill himself leaping after illusions. "Movie magic," he says. "People expect you to do things you just can't do."

Yet he remains an American icon, a living Elvis, larger than life. "I created the character called Evel Knievel," he says, "and he sort of got away from me.

"When I was performing, I thought I'd get killed. But, s---, I'm not ready to die today."

"He's not dying right now; if he was, he'd be in intensive care in the hospital," says Hector C. Ramos, director of liver transplantation for LifeLink and Tampa General Hospital. "But he definitely needs a liver transplant. I'm not sure if he'll last a year. Six months, I don't know. Definitely he'll last a month. At least I hope so; it'll take more than that to get a liver. We have anywhere from 15 to 25 percent of our patients die waiting for organs."

There will be one there for him when he needs it, Knievel says. "I've got to think positive. I mean, I never went into a jump thinking, "What if ?' "

'I knew I could draw a big crowd'

He was born Robert Craig Knievel in Butte, Mont., and raised by his grandparents after his parents separated in his first year. He picked up the nickname "Evil" in his hubcap-swiping days as a kid. (Some stories say he got it from the way he glared at pitchers during Little League games. Either way, the fact that it rhymed with his last name didn't hurt.)

Years later he changed the spelling and made it his legal name.

He married his high school girlfriend. Linda Bork was 16, he was 19, and he held what Linda said was "a different job every month - selling cars, selling insurance, selling graves."

He was 27 when he co-founded a motorcycle shop at Moses Lake, Wash. He wanted to attract more than just the typical motorcyclist. A jump might do it - say a 40-foot jump over a box of rattlesnakes with a mountain lion tethered at one end. It drew a crowd of about 1,000. After a few wheelies, he launched himself, came up short and landed on the box. It split open, snakes took off in every direction and so did most of the crowd. But those who didn't flee mobbed Knievel for autographs.

"Right then," he said, "I knew I could draw a big crowd by jumping over weird stuff."

A jump over two cars became a jump over five, then 10, then more. "It wasn't 'One day he's selling motorcycles and the next day Caesars Palace,' " Linda Knievel said from Butte. "It started out small and just grew. I was happy he'd finally found a job he liked."

She raised their children pretty much on her own. Their oldest son, Kelly, is 37, married and in sales. Robbie, a year younger, is unmarried with two daughters and has picked up where Dad left off, a daredevil motorcyclist. Tracey is 34, married, a stay-at-home mom with four children and a fifth on the way. Alicia, 19 and with a 1½-year-old daughter, lives with Linda in Butte.

The relationship with his children, cool for many years, has thawed, Linda said. "It's getting better. What he really loves is being a grandfather."

She doesn't wish Evel ill, she said, even after decades of his infidelities and a December divorce that ended their 38-year marriage. "I don't know why it never worked out. I guess maybe he always thought there was something better out there and never stopped looking for it."

'I can't do it'

The helmet is scarred, rubbed raw down to the inner liner. Knievel wore it once, when he jumped the fountains at Caesars Palace in Las Vegas 30 years ago. He cleared the fountains, bounced the landing on the far ramp. The impact tore the handlebars from his grip.

The slow-motion film seems endless, this rag doll of a man in his white leather jumpsuit tumbling, tumbling, tumbling. A fractured skull, broken pelvis, hip and ribs were only the most serious of the injuries. He was unconscious for nearly a month. But he was now in the consciousness of an American public that lusted after larger-than-life heroes.

"Promoters would say, 'You jumped 12 cars in Bakersfield; you've got to jump 15 for me.' I just went further and further." After a demolition derby in the Los Angeles Coliseum, Knievel took off from a ski-style ramp and jumped 52 wrecks at midfield.

"I think 75 percent of the people came to see me because they were fans, maybe 20 percent because if there was going to be an accident they wanted to see it, and 5 percent - the sick ones - who were looking for me to get killed," he said.

For years he had talked about jumping the Grand Canyon (the federal government objected). In 1974 he tried the 1,600-foot-wide Snake River Canyon in Idaho. It was part circus, part revival meeting, part Woodstock, part biker reunion - and pure Evel.

In front of 15,000 spectators and countless more watching on pay-per-view TV, his 13-foot-long Sky-Cycle X-2 lifted off from a 108-foot launch ramp, and a drogue parachute deployed prematurely. The main chute opened moments later and the X-2, blown back over the chasm, floated down, crashed into a side of the canyon and landed about 20 feet from the river. Knievel was unhurt.

He also was unsuccessful. No matter. On Sept. 9, 1974, he shared front-page headlines with ""Ford pardons Nixon." Snake River Canyon earned Knievel about $3-million and a niche in American lore.

There would be more stunts - and more fractures and concussions: crash-landing after clearing 13 double-decker London buses at Wembley Stadium, 14 Greyhound buses at King's Island, Ohio (which gave ABC's Wide World of Sports its highest-ever rating) and a tank of live sharks in Chicago.

There also would be 14 major operations, 35 broken bones, aluminum-alloy plates in his arms, a titanium hip and countless pins in every limb. He has spent 36 months in hospitals.

"I remember once I was in a restaurant - I was in a booth so nobody saw me - and one guy says how he saw me jump 100 cars in L.A. And the next guy says he was there when I jumped the Grand Canyon," Knievel said.

"The truth was getting stretched so much out of proportion about me that I began to think, 'I'm going to end up killing myself to try to be what these people want me to be. I can't do it.' That's when I decided to quit." His last jump was in 1980, with Robbie.

Evel Knievel became a gladiator with nothing left to conquer. For a few years he drank himself through his depression. He spent six months in jail after using a baseball bat on a former publicist who had written an unfavorable book about him.

He had always loved golf. It became a second high-stakes career. He would play 18 holes with $100,000 riding on the score. "It's a matter of carrying on something that gives you a knot in your stomach and a lump in your throat. That's what makes me feel good."

In the 1980s, Evel Knievel became something of an American afterthought. Robbie was, and is, jumping farther (he successfully jumped the Caesars Palace fountains in 1989), but like Pete Rose Jr. or Frank Sinatra Jr., Robbie Knievel is doomed to be nothing more than a pale imitation of greatness.

In the '90s, everything old is new again. And so is Evel Knievel. The current generation is discovering him; previous ones are re-kindling memories. He has become a hot commodity. He speaks often to youngsters about the wisdom of bicycle and motorcycle safety and the destructiveness of alcohol and drugs. With the endorsement deals and public appearances, he says, he's making $300,000 a year.

Out of the fast lane

Knievel lives with Krystal Kennedy in her Feather Sound condominium. There are a few of his paintings (he is accomplished in oils), including one of him in mid-jump, the Caesars Palace helmet on a shelf, a red, white and blue guitar from his good friend Buck Owens to "the coolest dude on planet earth," and, in the unfinished second bedroom, stacks of cartons, a year or more worth of fan mail and old and new Evel Knievel toys and games.

Kennedy is 27, sprightly, with a quick laugh. They have been together nearly seven years. If he ever marries again, Knievel says, it will be to her.

She played golf at Osceola High and Florida State University. A mutual friend introduced them at a local charity golf tournament. She had known Knievel's name, not much else. Her father, she said, was more excited than she was that she had met him.

"Until the last year or two," Kennedy says, seated on the couch, enveloping his right hand in her arms, "we lived a lot faster life. Drank a lot. A lot. Out every night 'til 3-4 in the morning."

They lived from city to city then, hotel to hotel, driving from one appearance to the next. "They know us in every bar in Atlanta and Chicago, and Dallas, Fort Worth and Houston, and L.A. and especially Hollywood by our first names," he says.

"It was bad for his temperament," she adds. "Now, if we're out one night a week for dinner, we've met our quota."

They spend months at a time in Las Vegas and often visit Butte.

He is never without a roll of $100 bills and rarely lets a day go by without betting $1,000 or more. He wears a diamond-encrusted ring that could double as a paperweight, and gold jewelry. When he's not riding his motorcycle ("I just put a new turbocharger on it, delivers 125 horsepower to the rear wheel"), he's driving a black Aston Martin Lagonda or a Chevy Tahoe with a trailer hitch for the motorcycle.

A .44 Magnum accompanies him when he drives at night. "I'd rather have 12 jurors judge me," he says, "than have six men carrying me to the grave." His hefty gold-and-ebony cane once held a sword, "but it made airport security crazy."

He says he has made $35-million in his career and has spent most of it. "If God meant you to hang onto money, he'd have put handles on it so you could drag it around," he says - but in the next breath he adds: "I spent a lot of money that I shouldn't have spent. Instead of buying one Lear jet, I bought two. Instead of buying one racehorse, I bought half a dozen. Instead of buying one ship, I bought 11 ...

"I've put away for my kids, my grandchildren and my wife. Linda's a wonderful woman." They speak by phone just about every other day. Their marriage was all but technically over long before he met Kennedy.

"Our marriage - she says like it says in the Bible, we were 'unequally yoked.' She knew I was a very promiscuous person. I'm not proud of it."

He pauses.

"It couldn't have been easy being married to Evel Knievel," he says.

It wasn't. "I knew he was with women, sleeping with them every night," Linda Knievel says. "I didn't ask for a divorce all that time because I was raised that when you got married you stayed married, and that's the way it was. I didn't want stepmoms and stepdads around, and I didn't want to be alone."

The divorce, she says, was Krystal's idea, "and that's fine. I'm happy he's found someone who loves him."

Since December he has played only a few nine-hole rounds of golf. He hasn't picked up a paintbrush in months. Krystal pesters him to do more. "It's tough to get motivated," he says. "I might not live. I'm concentrating on living."

We envision Evel Knievel outlined against the sky, forever flying. But there are days, sometimes a week at a time, he can't get out of bed.

(June 21, 1998)

~ Evel Knievel married Krystal Kennedy in 1999; they divorced in 2001 but remained together with homes in Clearwater and Butte. Also in 1999 he underwent a liver transplant. He was in failing health for years with diabetes and an incurable lung disease, idiopathic pulmonary fibrosis. He died November 30, 2007. He was 69. ~

Twenty-two

Casey down again; thanks, scab men

(Note: This was written in anticipation of Major League Baseball opening the 1995 season with replacement players. Two days after it appeared the 232-day strike ended. It had begun on August 12, 1994, wiping out 948 games plus the entire postseason.)

The outlook wasn't brilliant for the major leagues that day,
The rosters full of frauds who said they actually could play.
The sky was blue, the grass was green, the foul lines straight and white,
But under, on and 'twixt them was a terrifying sight.

The umpire, a replacement too, came out and said, "Play ball!"
He'd worked some games in Double A a month before last fall.
And from the home-team dugout came the motliest of mobs;
A pitcher who had spent a decade working at odd jobs.

A shortstop wearing spectacles. His teammates called him "Owl."
A catcher with a broken thumb. He'd tried to catch a foul.
A centerfielder, young and bright and full of vim and verve,
Who hit the fastball constantly but couldn't touch the curve.

The second sacker was a slacker, batting .101.
He'd spent two years in Leavenworth. He was the owner's son.
The dugout and the bullpen, with players both were full,
But truth be told, the manager was mostly full of bull.

"They're just as good as any lads that I have played before."
That they were mediocre was a fact he could ignore.
"They hit, they run, they catch, they throw, just like the other guys."
His comprehensive compliments were just a pack of lies.

"My boys can win the pennant," he then said without a smirk,
As he began a season of the owner's dirty work.
And as the players took the field and each took his position,
The fans sensed they were witnessing a loathsome new tradition.

Attendance in the stadium was nowhere near capacity,
The citizens expressing doubts about the club's veracity.
The few who came said 'twas a shame they couldn't cheer their heroes.
The cut-rate price was nice, they said, but still these guys were zeros.

The national anthem, normally sung by some recording star,
Was played instead by a guy named Fred from some piano bar.
And throwing out the ball was not some Hall of Fame-type player,
But the nephew of a councilman, a replacement for the mayor.

And when the game itself began, the fans reached the conclusion
That calling this thing major-league was simply self-delusion.
Each hit and catch was greeted by a brief, half-hearted cheer.
Some angry fans got semi-drunk from gulping down near-beer.

The opening inning took an hour, due mostly to the walks.
All nine of them, plus five hit batters, two fights and four balks.
The next three innings raced right by _ if you call two hours "racy."
And from the stands came this mournful chant, "Please give us back our
Casey."

And where was Casey? Where was Cal? And Rafael and Wade?
Where were our heroes, all of them, while this travesty was played?
Out chasing down endorsement deals, or driving their Mercedes,
Or getting on their families' nerves, or flirting with the ladies,

Or playing golf or catching bass or sunning in their yard,
Or signing scads of autographs (at seven bucks a card),
Or hastening this grand game's death, and wond'ring, what's the fuss?
But not going to legitimate jobs just like the rest of us.

Some guy we've never heard of is patrolling Ozzie's yard.
Another one on Roger's mound is throwing kind of hard.
And one stands right where Will belongs, recording outs at first.
In its entirety this is baseball we can call the worst.

A sneer is curling all our lips, our teeth are clenched in hate.
As much as hockey thrills us, it's a game without a plate.
As much as basketball excites us, and football in some cases,
Neither is a pastoral sport, and neither played with bases.

To a baseball fan, no tennis, golf or bowling stirs a glimmer
Of the passion that was fashioned by an Aaron or a Zimmer.
We won't ever care one whit about these frauds, these drips, these drabs.
For a nation's baseball fever can't be cured or healed by scabs.

– With apologies to Casey, and Ernest L. Thayer

(March 20, 1995)

Private Lives

Twenty-three

In my element... out of my league

The rite of passage can take many forms. For one sports writer on the road, it came in the form of a gregarious compatriot dragging him into the company of idols.

It was the winter of '72, my first season as No. 1 writer on the NFL beat for The Associated Press. I'd been a general assignments writer/ political writer/sports writer in Los Angeles, Sacramento and New York since joining The AP in 1967.

I had covered (albeit peripherally) presidents - the Lyndon Johnson "support-the-war" tour and Richard Nixon's flights to the Western White House, a governor (Reagan), an assassination (Bobby Kennedy at the Ambassador Hotel), a gruesome crime (the Tate-LaBianca murders by Charles Manson's minions), chaos (disturbances in Watts and an earthquake), and Super Bowl VI after the 1971 season.

Through all of that I was in my element but felt out of my league.

As The AP's Pro Football Writer in '72, there I was covering some Giants games, some Jets games and some road games in Pittsburgh, Miami, Dallas and elsewhere. And I was a loner, painfully shy.

I could ask questions of Angela Davis, Mario Savio, Ronald Reagan and Don Shula, but I felt myself an outsider among other writers. My afternoons and evenings before and after NFL games were spent in the shadows. I didn't belong. Not with these people. Not with Red Smith and Jim Murray and Dave Anderson. What could I say that could possibly interest them? Did they know who I was? Did they care?

While other writers on the road decided where to dine, I grabbed fast food and headed for my hotel room or went to a movie. Sometimes I still do.

My worst night on the road? Dallas, New Year's Eve, 1971. I was going to cover the 49ers-Cowboys game on Jan. 2. Why not, my editor suggested, help out at the Cotton Bowl on New Year's Day? I arrived in Dallas around 7 p.m. on Dec. 31 and called The AP bureau to tell them where I was staying.

"Hey, a few of the boys are havin' a party downtown," one of the bureau's sports writers drawled. "Wanna come?" Sure. I took down the name of the hotel and, at 9 p.m., put on a sport jacket and slacks and walked the five blocks.

The "boys" were the Cotton Bowl Committee. Black tie. Gentlemen in tuxedos; ladies in ball gowns. I didn't even make it to the lobby. I turned around, headed back to my hotel room, picked up a few chili burgers on the way, watched the ball descend in Times Square (on one-hour tape delay) and went to sleep.

Now it was nearly a year later, and I was still a recluse on the road. I was in Washington. The Cowboys-Redskins conference championship game was still a few days away. I was in a mostly empty press room in the hotel, finishing a story. Another writer stuck his head in the room.

"What are you doing for dinner?" he asked.

"Nothing."

"Mind if I join you?"

I sort of knew Dave Klein from covering Giants games. He was a columnist for the Newark Star-Ledger, and he was a big, bearded, boisterous bear of a man, very much my opposite. We'd said hello a few times. Actually, he'd said hello a few times. I just sort of waved or something.

Had he asked if I wanted to join him for dinner, I'd have muttered an excuse, an apology, and that would be that. But "Mind if I join you?" How could I say I minded? I said okay.

He left. Five minutes later he was back.

"Umm, there might be a few more people? Is that all right?"

I nodded.

"Let's meet in the lobby in half an hour."

The few more people were Dave Anderson, sports columnist for the New York Times (in 1981 he would win the Pulitzer Prize); Mo Seigel, sports columnist for the Washington Star and a master raconteur; William N. Wallace, football writer for the New York Times; John Scali, the White House special consultant for foreign affairs and communications (and a year away from replacing George Bush as permanent U.S. representative to the United Nations), and Edward Bennett Williams, high-powered lawyer and majority owner of the Washington Redskins.

Them.

And me.

We must have hit half a dozen restaurants and bars, crossing paths with other journalists and broadcasters, players and team owners, the glitterati of the sport, the nation and its capital.

Klein and Anderson and the rest ... and especially Seigel ... told stories, one after the other, about great people and great games, recollections about writers, athletes and events that could never be printed anywhere.

At first I held back, laughing along with the rest of them, nursing a drink and wondering what the hell I was doing in this crowd. After a while, though, someone told a story that triggered one from me, about Reagan and his California henchmen.

And a little later, about the time Yogi Berra went wild when ...

And sometime after that, the time...

The night didn't end until 3 in the morning. Maybe later.

I couldn't believe it.

I was one of them.

The next morning the pack of sports writers headed out for more player interviews. I caught up to Klein.

"You have no idea what you did for me last night," I said.

"I know *exactly* what I did for you last night," he said ... and proceeded to tell me about a young, scared sports writer who didn't dare try to mingle with the hotshot bylines of the early '60s, until Harold Rosenthal, a gentle fellow sports writer for the New York Herald-Tribune, had stuck his head into a press room and asked, "What are you doing for dinner? ... Mind if I join you?"

Klein had been welcomed into the circle. He belonged. And he swore he would pay Rosenthal back by doing the same thing for some other insecure, nervous sports writer. And he had.

There's another one out there. I haven't found him yet. But I will.

I owe it to Dave.

(January 10, 1996)

⌇ *Dave Klein retired from the Star Ledger in 1995 after 41 years. For 15 years he was editor and publisher of The Giants Newsweekly a subscription newspaper, then founded E-GIANTS.net, a subscription Internet publication. Klein is one of only three sportswriters who have covered every Super Bowl game. He has written more than 20 books, both fiction and non-fiction.* ⌇

Twenty-four

Curses, Rangers are foiled again

NEW YORK - Dunkirk happened, and the Germans marched down the Champs Elysees, and Jack Nicklaus and Mario Andretti and Pele were born, and so was the Jeep, and Emma Goldman and Marcus Garvey and Leon Trotsky died, and the HMS Queen Elizabeth arrived in New York for the first time . . .

. . . and the Stanley Cup arrived in New York for the last time. And if you are a New York Rangers fan, that is all 1940 means to you.

And the curse continues.

The Rangers have won the NHL's most prized possession three times, but never in front of their own fans. They had the glorious opportunity in Game 5 Thursday night to right that wrong. They didn't. They can win it 2,920 miles from home Saturday night in the Pacific Coliseum. And somehow that just won't seem fair.

And if they don't win it in Vancouver they can win it Tuesday night in Madison Square Garden.

But all Ranger fans who absolutely, positively knew they were going to win it in five will be equally certain in their hearts that New York is going to lose it in seven, that the Canucks are going to steal the Cup, and that the most important goal in Rangers' history will still belong to Bryan Hextall 54 years ago in Toronto.

If you are a Boston Red Sox fan, if you are a Chicago Cubs fan … if, for that matter, you are a Tampa Bay Bucs fan … you understand the curse.

If you curse Bill Buckner for letting a grounder get away, or Leon Durham for letting a grounder get away, or Hugh Culverhouse for letting Doug Williams get away, well, maybe in the grand scheme of things you simply haven't suffered enough.

In the nearly 30 years between the Rangers' last Stanley Cup and the NHL's first expansion, there were only six teams in the league and four made the playoffs, and all anyone had to do was win eight games for the championship. Now all anyone has to do is win 16. New York has won 15. To a Rangers fan, that's not even close.

This Curse of the Cup is as palpable to Rangers fans as Harry Frazee's decision to sell Babe Ruth to the Yankees is to Red Sox fans. It is a curse grounded in history, and the villain is John Reed Kilpatrick, or Red Dutton, or Fred Shero.

Kilpatrick was one of the bosses of the old Garden. After the Rangers won the Cup, the mortgage on the building was paid off and, in a time-honored tradition, Kilpatrick burned the mortgage.

In the Cup.

If Kilpatrick's using the sport's most treasured trophy as an ashtray wasn't the start, then Dutton's proclamation was. He was manager of the New York Americans, an NHL team that rented the Garden ice.

When the Garden saw how profitable they were, they formed their own team, the Rangers, and put the squeeze on the Americans by raising the rent and taking all the best dates for themselves.

The Americans went out of business in 1942 and Dutton angrily proclaimed: "The Rangers will never win the Cup again in my lifetime!" He died in 1987.

Then there was Shero. He coached the Rangers in 1979, the last time they got this close to the Cup. Shero loved to party, and Montreal is a wonderful place to party.

The Rangers won the opener, taking away the Canadiens' home-ice advantage. Shero went out to celebrate that night and the next, and so did the Rangers. They didn't win another game.

Maybe going up three games to one this year is just another message to Ranger fans that they haven't suffered enough.

Maybe if the Canucks don't score with a minute left in the third period of Game 1 and win it in overtime, or if New York doesn't have a goal taken away in Game 5 by a phantom offside call, then maybe Rangers fans haven't suffered enough.

Maybe if the Islanders don't win four Stanley Cups and lord it over the Rangers, and maybe if the Mets and Jets and Knicks don't win world championships while the Rangers fail and fail and fail again, then maybe their fans haven't suffered enough.

I feel sorry for Cowboys fans. They have no idea what it is like to really suffer. Super Bowls come too easy to them. Same thing with Montrealers. They go a few years without a Cup, then they win another one. They have won 24, too many to understand how precious it is.

Fifty-four years and counting.

(June 10, 1994)

~ In Vancouver on Saturday, June 11, the Canucks defeated the Rangers 4-1, tying the best-of-seven Stanley Cup finals at three games apiece. ~

Twenty-five

This fan's Cup dream comes true

NEW YORK - So there was no curse, after all. There was simply time waiting for talent. Nothing in sports is forever except victory. They can never take that away from you.

And eventually... finally... it happens, even for a city in which paranoia is a lifestyle and terror everyone's significant other.

New York owns the Stanley Cup, Brian Leetch owns the Conn Smythe Trophy as the playoffs' Most Valuable Player, the most important goal in the Rangers' history belongs to Mark Messier, and Bryan Hextall's goal for them 54 years ago in overtime in Toronto is relegated to the dustbin of minutiae.

And 1940 is just another year, the year Thomas Wolfe's book *You Can't Go Home Again* was published.

Actually, you can.

I did, consummating a love affair that predates puberty.

All the energy invested in the unrequited love of Gump Worsley and Eddie Giacomin is now worth it, and for the moment this dirty, noisy, crumbling, arrogant gotham has never looked more like Oz to someone who grew up here.

The Rangers took possession of my heart and soul in 1954 … and they were not going to win the Cup this year without me. Not after all I had been through with them when the NHL was six teams and my mood swung on the success or failure of Andy Bathgate and Dean Prentice and Camille Henry.

If my nephew and his fiancee had decided to be wed in July, I would have been just another distant Stanley Cup observer.

But Mickey and Jen chose Memorial Day weekend in New York; family obligations sent me here, rather than to Indianapolis to write about an automobile race.

Even before the season ended, I counted off the playoff dates. The wedding was May 29; the Stanley Cup Finals began May 31. "The Rangers will win the Cup," I announced, "they will win it at home, and I will be there to see it."

Friends and colleagues warned me about building my expectations too high, about disrupting the karma.

Well, I have spent my entire life being cautious, not getting too excited for fear of being too disappointed. I'm sorry, I told them, but I have died too many deaths with this team to not have it be a part of me now.

And with the indulgence of a somewhat understanding and slightly bemused editor, I remained in New York while my very understanding and vastly bemused wife and children went home.

And I covered the games in Madison Square Garden and kept 40 years of emotion bottled up within me.

Until Tuesday night, when I sought out Alan Drogy, whom I seem to have known forever, and his twin sons, Leon and Barry, and stood with them in Row F of Sec. 303 as the game's final, agonizing seconds wound down, releasing four decades of frustration.

And the people chanted "Nineteen-forty" over and over again, and as Messier and Leetch and goalie Mike Richter and all the fans' gods circled the ice, holding aloft the NHL's most treasured trophy, the chant turned to "Nineteen Ninety-four!" and the people broke open splits of champagne and sipped from their own miniature Stanley Cups.

The streets surrounding the Garden after the game had a V-J Day feel … although the threat of mayhem hung heavy, big-city championship celebrations being flint for vandals these days.

The Garden, littered with debris, is now littered with memories.

And, yes, they will be able to sweep out the former in time for a basketball game tonight, but they will never be able to dispose of the latter.

In the grand scheme of things, the Rangers' winning on Tuesday night means nothing. It will not change my life one whit, nor will it make this city or the world a better place to live … and I'm sorry, but for the moment it is to me absolutely the most important thing in the universe.

And I will get over it all too quickly.

Yes, the Rangers have the Stanley Cup, and if victory is forever, it also is ephemeral. The pleasure of winning is exceeded tenfold, a hundredfold, by the pain of losing.

They are champions today, and come next year they will find new and sinister ways to break their fans' hearts. And if they win the Cup next year, too, it won't be the same. Not for me.

You always remember your first.

I am through with the Rangers now. I have carried them long enough. My demons are exorcised. Let someone else suffer.

(June 15, 1994)

⌒ The New York Rangers returned to the Stanley Cup Finals in 2014, losing in five games to the Los Angeles Kings. ⌒

179

Twenty-six

He played his part in Dodgers history

TAMPA - Sandy Amoros, his right leg propped up, sits alone, reading a baseball magazine. The television, as usual, is on, the sound turned down to a murmur. It is that way every day in his three-room apartment in west Tampa. It was that way every day for a couple of weeks last month in his room at Tampa General Hospital.

Life has not been terribly kind to this Cuban native who a generation ago had the world in the palm of his outstretched glove. He was 25 when he reached out and made the catch that helped give the Brooklyn Dodgers their only world championship.

Now he is 61, slender, bespectacled. He lost part of his left leg to amputation four years ago. Today, his right one bears the scars of recent surgery. He says he is losing feeling in his fingers.

"Things are not so bad," he says. "Really."

For virtually all of his brief major-league career, Amoros was a bit player, hardly in the same league with most of the Boys of Summer.

But on Oct. 4, 1955, he became as much a hero as any Brooklyn has ever had.

"The Dodgers, they the best team," Amoros said with obvious warmth in his heavily accented English. "Very nice people. They talk to me like they know me for a very long time. Very nice."

His smile widened. "The Brooklyn Bums … Pee Wee, Duke, Furillo, Campanella, Robinson, Hodges, Gilliam, Erskine, Labine, Black, Newcombe, Podres …

"But when I get to Brooklyn, they make me crazy. Before, when I swing the bat, I hit it everywhere. They throw outside, I hit it to left; they throw inside, I pull the ball to right; they throw it up the middle, I hit it up the middle. They say, 'You hit home runs. Go for the scoreboard.' " It was 297 feet down the rightfield line, where the 40-foot Schaefer scoreboard loomed. " 'You hit it to Bedford Avenue,' they tell me."

With Brooklyn, Amoros never batted higher than .277, never hit more than 16 home runs in a season. But on that afternoon in Yankee Stadium …

If Amoros is weary of talking about that one serendipitous moment - the sixth inning of the seventh game of the '55 World Series - he doesn't show it. He will willingly, if not enthusiastically, recount it.

Brooklyn led the Yankees 2-0 and Dodgers manager Walter Alston had to shuffle his defense after having sent George Shuba up to bat for Don Zimmer. With Zimmer gone, Alston moved Junior Gilliam from leftfield to second base and sent Amoros out to left.

Johnny Podres walked Billy Martin to lead off the bottom of the sixth, Gil McDougald singled and, with runners on first and second, Yogi Berra punched a high-outside fastball down the leftfield line.

"I wasn't trying to hit it there," Berra said from his Bloomfield, N.J., home. "I had two strikes on me. I was just guarding the plate."

Amoros, shading the left-handed Berra well over to left-center, took off at the crack of the bat. "He just kept on running and when he got near the railing, he slammed on the brakes," McDougald said from his home in Spring Lake, N.J. "When he did that, I figured there was no way he could catch the ball. But he stuck out his glove quickly and it was like he found an Easter egg in it."

The Dodgers said then - and Podres, now the Phillies' pitching coach, and Berra and McDougald all still agree - that the slower, right-handed Gilliam wouldn't have been able to make the catch, that the ball would have fallen in for an extra-base hit, that one run would certainly have scored, probably two. And with nobody out, two runs in and a runner in scoring position ...

But Amoros not only made the catch. He wheeled and threw the ball to shortstop Pee Wee Reese, who relayed it to Gil Hodges at first, just barely doubling up McDougald.

"Saved the game for them," Berra said. "We're lucky it wasn't a triple play."

The Yankees' threat was extinguished. Podres shut them out the rest of the way. "Lucky," Amoros said of his heroics. "Just lucky... Johnny Podres. Great pitcher."

Podres, told of Amoros' comment, grunted. "He doesn't make that catch and we don't win that game. Simple as that. He's the hero."

And McDougald, the victim, said good-naturedly: "It'd have been more heroic if he'd run into the fence and dropped the ball."

Amoros was supposed to be the next Willie Mays, a fleet outfielder who could hit both for average and power. He batted .337 with 19 home runs for St. Paul in 1952 and an International League-leading .353 with 23 homers for Montreal in 1953.

He had a funny wiggle to his bat as he waited for the pitch. It was his trademark. It could have become as famous as Stan Musial's corkscrew stance or Juan Marichal's high kick.

But that catch in 1955 was Amoros' first and last moment of stardom. "I don't do nothing after that," he said.

He had one last chance at glory almost exactly a year later. On Oct. 8, 1956, in the fifth inning of the fifth game of the World Series, with the Yankees leading Brooklyn 1-0, he walloped a drive high and deep to rightfield. But it curved foul - just foul - at the last moment. Amoros wound up as just one of the 27 outs in Don Larsen's perfect game.

In 1960 the Dodgers traded him to Detroit. The Tigers sold him to Denver of the American Association in 1961. By 1962, the only venue left for him was the Mexican League. After that, nothing.

He returned home, where he was still a hero, a Cuban who had made it to the majors and had made a difference. Fidel Castro asked Amoros to manage one of the teams in a professional summer league he had formed.

Amoros wanted to keep playing in Mexico. Castro told Amoros to manage. Amoros declined. Castro didn't let him out of the country. Amoros couldn't get a job. For nearly five years he barely left his house. He divorced and remarried.

In 1967, when Amoros and more than 60,000 other Cubans were permitted to leave the country, he and his wife and their daughter migrated to Miami. He was destitute. "A small ranch, an old car, that is all I had," Amoros said. "The government, they keep it. I lost everything."

When he left baseball, he was one week short of the minimum five years he needed to qualify for a major-league pension. Buzzie Bavasi, then the Dodgers' general manager, was told of Amoros's plight and signed him to a one-week contract, then Amoros moved to New York.

His second wife divorced him. A decade of menial jobs and unemployment later, in 1977, Amoros moved to Tampa and began receiving his $840-a-month baseball pension.

By then, he was losing feeling in his toes. Now there was pain, sometimes intolerable. Smoking and inactivity had taken their toll on his circulatory system. In 1987, his left leg was amputated below the knee.

Last month he had more surgery - the Baseball Alumni Team (BAT), founded to help indigent former players, picked up the bills -

to restore circulation in his right leg. "This one, the same problem as that one," Amoros said. "I probably lose this one someday, too. That's what they told me."

Next month, he said, he plans to accept his daughter's invitation to move in with her in Miami, to spend time with two of his four grandchildren (the other two are in Cuba with his first wife).

"One of them, he is 12," Amoros said. "He told me once he'll be a ballplayer. That's good."

(April 24, 1991)

Sandy Amoros died of pneumonia on June 27, 1992, in Miami.

Twenty-seven

On the ball

HAINES CITY - The sun is high over court No. 8 at the Rick Macci International Tennis Academy at Grenelefe.

On an adjoining court, Macci is refining a young man's service.

Nearby, an oversized portable radio blasts rock music.

On No. 8, Stefano Capriati stands, racket in hand, beside a shopping cart filled with yellow tennis balls. He is muscular but with a prominent gut.

"When you play a lot of sports and then you don't do it so much ..." he says in his thick Italian accent.

Sweat pastes his polo shirt to his back.

On the other side of the net is Jennifer, his daughter. Baggy T-shirt and draw-string shorts. Barrettes and a ponytail. Pearl earrings and chewing gum.

"Adjust your feet," Stefano says.

Jennifer, standing at the baseline, stares back and pops her gum.

Her father, four tennis balls in hand, hits one to her right, another to her left as she volleys, another to her right as she rushes the net, then lobs one high over her head.

After the overhand smash, she trudges back to the baseline, the pigeon-toed, head-down walk of boredom.

Four more balls, another charge toward the net, four more returns. "Attack!" her father is yelling. "Feet! Feet!" With every swing, an "ungh!" escapes from Jennifer's throat. The trademark of the tennis champion.

Another trudge to the baseline. Four more balls, four more volleys, four more grunts. Another trudge. He is pointing out her mistakes, mixing criticism with praise. She doesn't acknowledge him, but she hears him.

"Perfect!" he says after her next rush. Then she bashes a lob 10 feet beyond the baseline.

"No, no, Jenny," he says kindly as she giggles. "Do well."

"Da-ad," she says in the sing-song of petulance, indulgence. "What's the big deal?"

"You do that in exercises," he says, "you do it in matches."

Four more balls, four more volleys, four more grunts ...

Twenty minutes later, they take a break. A brief one. She takes a drink, he gathers up the dozens of balls littering the court and refills the shopping cart. She returns to the baseline. He picks up four balls.

Jennifer Capriati was born to tennis, literally.

"When I was pregnant," Denise Capriati said, "I played until the very last day. Ten days after she was born, I was back on the court, playing to get back into shape. She was right there on the court with me, in a basket. When she started crawling, it was on the court, pushing a ball around. When she got old enough, she started picking up balls for me. Then she picked up a racket and started swinging it."

She hasn't stopped since. Jennifer Capriati is 12 now and already the winner of this year's U.S. Tennis Association Hard Court and Clay Court championships in the 18-and-under division.

She says she's ready to turn pro "soon." Two years, she says. Three at the outside. "I'm always thinking about it. Always."

They are standing together at the baseline now. The sun has moved to their left. He has showed her what he wants in a serve, and now she is serving ball after ball. Some of them fly into the net. Some sail beyond the opposite baseline. Some are clean serves.

Finally, Jennifer tries to cut a deal. If she can make five good serves in a row, this lesson will be over. It takes a dozen serves before Stefano even agrees.

Good. Good. Fault. Start over.

Eleven serves later, she is finished.

"Even when I mess up, he's happy when the mechanics are right," she says, gazing at her father. "He's not that hard to please. All he wants is for me to do everything right." She is not being sarcastic.

As tired as she is after a couple of hours of practice, she says she will never tire of tennis. "It's still fun, all the time. The main thing is to have fun, before any of the big stuff, when it starts getting serious," she says, wise beyond her years. "I know this is going to be my career, but I also want to be able to enjoy it, too."

She attends public school from 8 a.m. to 1 p.m. and practices her game from 2:30 to 6:30 p.m. Weekends are her own, unless she's in a tournament. She plans to attend college - although she says with a shrug that she's not exactly sure why.

Her life has been charted, both by her and for her. She will play tennis for money and fame.

When was the decision made? Who made it?

Jennifer just shrugs. It doesn't matter.

"I didn't decide," Stefano says, not a bit defensively.

Denise looks at him. "Before she was born," she says.

Well, yes, he says, he always hoped Jennifer would play tennis, "just to see if she would like it. If she didn't want to, I wouldn't push her. You push kids, lot of times the kids push back. To keep going, they must want it."

She has always been competitive. When Jennifer was 17 months old, her mother says, she won a swim competition against 5-year-olds. A few years ago her mother had to set limits on her swimming. Jennifer was developing the wrong muscles for a tennis player.

When she was 3, Stefano began hitting balls to his daughter. She started hitting them back right away, even before she really knew what tennis was.

Now, she says, tennis isn't the most important thing to her. "It's the only thing."

The only thing?

"Well, I mean, there's school (she is a straight-A student) and I like to go to Boardwalk and Baseball and stuff," she says. And she ice skates and swims. "But tennis is what I do."

Denise is 38, a flight attendant. Stefano, 53, used to be a soccer player and a stuntman. "We have this tape of 100 Rifles," Denise says. "He's wearing a beard and Raquel Welch shoots him off a train and 'There goes daddy!' "

Stefano is ostensibly retired now. He calls himself a tennis consultant. What he does is look for youngsters with potential, youngsters who might benefit from enrollment at a tennis academy.

The Capriatis used to live in Spain and would commute - sometimes together, sometimes not - to New York, Denise's base with Pan American.

The family moved to Lauderhill, near Fort Lauderdale, in 1980.

Jennifer was 5 when she began training at Holiday Park under the tutelage of Jimmy Evert, Chris's father.

At the start, Evert taught her twice a week while Stefano worked with her every day, first for 10 or 15 minutes, eventually for an hour or two.

"I could see at 5 that she had a lot of potential," Evert said. "She was hitting clean, solid groundstrokes. Every time she played, people would stop and watch."

There weren't any youngsters around at Holiday Park. She would play her father, or one of two college-age players. Every day she would lose. Frustration began to set in. Besides, there was no way to judge her against others at her own level. Then, through a friend, Stefano Capriati met Rick Macci.

Macci gathers some of his pupils for the next training session.

There are only 14 full-time youngsters in his program, most paying the $800-to-$1,800-a-month tuition (depending on whether housing is included) and 10 part-timers.

First, sprints on the court. Then to the grass. This could just as well be a football camp in miniature. The youngsters high-step through automobile tires. Hula hoops lie in rows, about six feet apart. The youngsters leap from one to the next. Other hoops form a tunnel. The youngsters crawl through them. Around and around and around, until they are ready to drop.

Macci keeps up non-stop chatter, encouragement and jokes leavened with deprecation. Then it's back to the courts, Macci with eight students on No. 7, his wife, Joy, with five on No. 6.

On No. 8, Stefano Capriati is coaching Jennifer's 9-year-old brother, Steven. "He is very athletic, too," Stefano says. "He loves to run. I don't know if he runs to play tennis or plays tennis to run."

He is good.

"He is going to be better."

Macci hits ball after ball across the net as the students, one by one, rush in for the return, trot to the net, tap it with the racket and head to the back of the line again.

Every few minutes, there are footwork drills - "alley cats," the students leaping sideways across the singles and doubles lines, and "shuffles," bounding sideways from one edge of the court to the other.

Always there is the chatter, Macci calling out the youngsters by their nicknames. Jennifer is Spark.

"World-class backhand, Smoke. That was an arrow. Defense. Run it down. Got to hurt 'em. Got to control the point. Pulling up too soon, Spike. Attitude, that's what gets you the free ride to UCLA, to Pepperdine ..."

Once in a while, Macci dumps a surprise ball to a corner of the court or barely over the net. The unsuspecting student lurches after it, sometimes missing, usually not.

"Have an answer, Chris. Don't bend from the waist. From the knee. React to the feet, Cat, not the hands. Cup of water on your head, Tom. You're not playing peewee anymore, Spark."

"I first saw her play in Fort Lauderdale," Macci said. "She was 9, this pint-sized kid hitting every ball, *every* ball, so aggressively. The racket was almost bigger than she was. I'd never seen anything like it.

"The way she was playing, trying to play, was what impressed me. She was attacking every ball, even if it was a foot over her head and she had to jump. Most kids just lob those back. That's what impressed me. She was, at 9, the most complete package of a tennis player I'd ever seen at that age."

For 14 months, Stefano packed the family into the car each weekend for the 3½-hour drive from Lauderhill to Grenelefe, so Jennifer could study under Macci. Last March they moved there.

"They were looking for better competition," Evert said. "It was the only move they could make."

The sun is approaching the horizon. The students are engaged in the day's final exercise, two-on-twos.

Spark and Spike (Brett Stern of Miami) are teamed against Smoke (Tommy Ho of Winter Haven) and Will Bull (he has no nickname; he's too new to have earned one - and Bull's not available. That's Steven Capriati's nickname). Two other doubles teams wait their turns in the round-robin competition.

Macci bounces tennis balls onto the court for one team or the other in a ferociously fast game of doubles, 11 points wins. If one team gets too big a lead, Macci tosses "bunnies" that the trailing team can blast for easy points.

Four losses eliminates a team. The last survivor is excused from wind sprints.

The instant each of her matches is over, Jennifer Capriati heads for a bench and hunches over a book. She is a voracious reader, a book every day or two. This one is an adolescent romance novel, *More Than Just a Smart Girl* ("When Alissa decides to skip eighth grade and start high school she wasn't at all sure she could handle it. After all, being smart doesn't always make you popular. But then she caught the eye of Rockwell High's football star …").

Capriati doesn't look up until it's her turn to return to the court.

Minutes later, exhausted, she and Cat (Sandy Surephong, from Baltimore) are giggling over a private joke. It is very easy, watching her in her element, in the heat of competitive tennis, to forget that she is only 12.

"She always wants to be No. 1," her father says. "She said it first, when she was maybe 7, 8. I didn't tell her she had to be. Matter of fact, when she said it, I told her how there'd be a lot of sacrifice. 'I know that.' She said it like she always knew."

She is headed off the court now when she is asked, What if someone told you that your tennis career was over, that you couldn't play anymore?

She takes the question at face value, answering it as any 12-year-old might.

"I'd cry," she says. "I'd be very unhappy and I'd ask why I wasn't allowed."

The question is rephrased: What if you tore up a leg and the doctor said you'd never play tennis again?

Jennifer Capriati pops her gum and stares back. "I'd start working on my comeback," she says.

(November. 13, 1988)

~ Jennifer Capriati turned pro on March 5, 1990; she was 13. By year's end she became the youngest player to be ranked in the Women's Tennis Association top ten. In 1992, at age 16, she defeated Steffi Graf at the Barcelona Olympics to win the gold medal. But by 1993 the pressure was getting to her. After losing in the first round of the U.S. Open she left the pro tennis tour, experimented with drugs and was arrested twice, for shoplifting and marijuana possession. She returned in 1996 but was minimally successful, occasionally reaching the semifinals of an event. Five years later, in 2001, she won the Australian Open, defeating defending champion Lindsay Davenport and top-ranked Martina Hingis in the semifinal and final rounds, She also won the 2001 French Open and 2002 Australian Open and became No. 1 in the world. The comeback didn't last. Serious and repeated injuries in 2003-2004 limited her play and at the end of 2004 she was forced into retirement by a right shoulder injury that surgery could not repair. ~

Twenty-eight

Still plenty of good seats available

B ASEBALL CITY, Fla. - The loudspeakers in the centerfield score-board play the traditional "Charge!" the sound of the trumpets sweeping across the field and washing over the stands.

Joyce Worrall pauses in midsentence.

"Charge!" she replies once, twice, three times.

She is the only one shouting. None of the other 87 fans has re-sponded. "I don't care," she says. "I'm here to cheer my boys on."

Her boys are the Baseball City Royals. Joyce and her daughter, Peggyann, and Rich Wharram have pretty much adopted the Florida State League team. They are season-ticket holders – the *only* season-ticket holders.

They never have those "guess-the-attendance' nights 'cause everyone could just go out and count 'em. Wouldn't be any fun.
- **Steve Otto, pitcher**

The Baseball City Royals play in the 8,000-seat centerpiece of the Kansas City Royals' spring-training and player-development facilities. When the major-league team leaves, so do the fans. The Class A team averages 117 fans a game at Baseball City Stadium.

Just across from the concession and souvenir stands, a locked gate with an "Amusement Park Closed" sign stretches across the promenade. Beyond it, the roller coaster and Ferris wheel loom silently, stark against the sky. They are symbolic tombstones.

When Anheuser-Busch Cos. Inc. bought six theme parks from Harcourt Brace Jovanovich Inc. (HBJ) last September and, four months later, closed Boardwalk and Baseball, it was like turning off a spigot. The flow - well, the trickle - of people into Baseball City Stadium virtually dried up.

We have this pool. We make our guess before the game, then we go out and count the house and see who's closest. – **Eddie Pierce, relief pitcher**

The Royals averaged 560 fans a game a year ago, hardly overwhelming but not the worst in the FSL. The Miami Miracle averaged 223.

This year, Winter Haven is second-lowest with 279 fans a game. St. Petersburg is tops with 2,200; the league average is 1,023.

Still, Winter Haven, St. Petersburg and the rest of the FSL teams sit in the communities from which they draw their steady fans. Baseball City, the unincorporated area surrounding the stadium, has a population of nine. So one-third of the residents are season-ticket holders. If the St. Petersburg Cardinals had the same percentage, they'd have 81,434 season-ticket holders.

The Royals draw from communities like Haines City, Davenport, Dundee, Lake Wales and Clermont, 10 to 30 miles away. Total population: barely 30,000.

"We're not doing anything different than they do in St. Petersburg or any other ballpark," says Karl Rogozenski, the Baseball City Royals' general manager. "We're still trying to get people to come out to the ballpark. It's just a little tougher for us."

"Most of these boys are from somewhere else. They don't have anybody. Maybe it's better to have small crowds. This way the players get to know a lot of people. We get to be family." - **Jean Pritchard of Dundee, a Royals booster**

The Baseball City Royals' 1989 attendance average wasn't based on what clubs call the "turnstile count." They didn't have any turnstiles. Fans who had paid their way into Boardwalk and Baseball could stroll over, watch a few innings (or the whole game) at no charge, and return to the amusement park.

HBJ sold platinum passes entitling bearers to get into its three theme parks (Boardwalk and Baseball, Sea World, and Cypress Gardens) for an entire year. Part of that package included the baseball games. In essence, the passes were season tickets for the Baseball City Royals.

"There were something like 200,000 passes out there," Rogozenski says. "If we'd counted 'em, we'd have had a million people for our first homestand and outdrawn the National League. But we're not trying to deceive anyone."

"The more people, the less you can actually hear when they holler at you. Usually it's just a lot of noise. Here you can hear every word and you can tell exactly who's saying it." - **Umpire Brian King**

Kevin Long breaks for home at the crack of the bat. The shortstop fields the ball and fires home, trapping Long in a rundown. As the Dunedin Blue Jays catcher charges toward him, Long dives to the ground.

"No, no! Missed him!" King shouts at the catcher, flinging his arms wide in the "safe" sign as Long scrambles to his feet and dashes home.

In an instant, Dennis Holmberg, the Dunedin manager, is in King's face.

"He got him!" Holmberg shouts.

"No he didn't!" King shouts back.

"Yes he did!" Holmberg shouts back.

You can hear them 200 feet away. Except for some clapping and chattering in the Royals' dugout, King's voice and Holmberg's voice are the only voices audible in Baseball City Stadium.

It's almost like a morgue, it's so quiet sometimes. Even when you score a run or something, you don't hear anything. You hit a home run, it's as though it never happened." - **Grant Griesser, catcher**

The Baseball City Royals' record crowd is 5,719. They set it June 16 against Lakeland – in Daytona Beach, which hasn't had an FSL team since 1986. It was a "home" game for the Royals, a fund-raiser to support youth baseball and help out a team of touring Soviet high school baseball players.

On June 8 the Royals staged Holiday Inn Night at Baseball City Stadium. As part of its advertising package, the hotel across from the deserted amusement park received several thousand tickets.

They were free for the asking at the front desk. That Friday night, 466 fans showed up. Other promotions haven't done as well. Helmet Day drew 54 fans.

Sometimes you can hear a bird cracking some peanut shells. - **Sean Collins, second baseman**

"We could just open the gates and let people in," Rogozenski says, "but this is still valuable entertainment and we don't want to cheapen the product. We put a price on it."

It's $3 for adults, $2 for senior citizens and children under 12; any seat in the house - except Joyce's and Peggyann's. The Worralls sit in Section 115, Row C, Seats 4-5, down the first-base line, fixtures under their big rainbow-colored umbrellas that shield them from the sun or the rain. All the players know them.

Joyce is 66, a resident of Davenport for 9½ years. When she married Rex 45 years ago in Detroit, she spent the first afternoon of her honeymoon in the bleachers at Briggs Stadium, watching a Tigers game. "Rex doesn't like baseball," Joyce says. "He's home, weeding the garden or something."

Several paper bags are nestled by Joyce Worrall's feet. She gives home-baked cookies to any Royals player who hits a home run or pitcher who goes at least five innings.

It's tempting to yell, 'Tracy, cut that out!' from 300 feet away. I bet I could, and I bet he'd hear me. - **Kevin Long, outfielder**

Kevin's wife, Marcey, brings their children, Tracy, 3, and Britney, 5, to just about every home game. "I'm out in leftfield, they're behind the plate, and I can see them. I can hear them. I know when the kids get in trouble. I can see Marcey spank 'em.

"I played at the University of Arizona. We'd play Stanford, UCLA, we'd have at least 4,000 a game. Last year in Eugene (Ore., the Royals' Class A team in the Northwest League), our average attendance was about 3,700. The kids would wander off and, with so many people there, half the time you'd lose 'em. My wife loves taking them to these games 'cause we can see everything they do.

"There's this song they play here where you're supposed to repeat the words. Nobody does it. We do it in the dugout - louder than the crowd."

You can hear somebody sneeze. - **Jacob Brumfield, outfielder**

Sean Collins is complaining good-naturedly. The second baseman started the season here, spent a month with the Appleton (Wis.) Foxes of the Class A Midwest League, then returned to Baseball City.

"No girls come to our games," he says. "It's bad. Nothing to look at in your free time. Usually you're taking ground balls and you look up and see a little cutie up there. You can't even do that. It's *ba-ad*. Baseball, baseball, baseball, that's all it is. This is definitely a job."

(June 29, 1990)

Steve Otto, Sean Collins and Grant Griesser never progressed beyond the lower-level minor leagues. Brian King spent seven years as a minor-league umpire. Eddie Pierce spent seven seasons in the minors and, in 1992, pitched in two games for the Kansas City Royals. From 1992-1999 Jacob Brumfield played for the Toronto Blue Jays, Cincinnati Reds, Pittsburgh Pirates and Los Angeles Dodgers. Kevin Long played for 10 minor league teams and in 1998-99 he managed two of Kansas City's Class-A teams in the minors. He never made to the majors – as a player. The New York Yankees named Long their hitting coach before the 2007 season and fired him on Oct. 10, 2014. Thirteen days later the New York Mets made Long their hitting coach.

Anheuser-Busch bought the theme park and stadium in 1989 and closed the theme park in 1990. Two years later the Baseball City Royals moved to Wilmington, Del. The ballpark remained the Kansas City Royals' spring training home until 2002. It was demolished in 2005.

Twenty-nine

When it's better to be last than first

LUTZ - The greeting was enthusiastic, albeit a bit underwhelming. Being No. 1, it turns out, is not necessarily all that rewarding.

The dew was still on the grass … and the grass beyond the first tee was pristine, with nary a new divot or golfer's spike marks … when Miller Barber, Rocky Thompson and Jim Holtgrieve teed off Sunday.

Someone has to go first, and it was Barber's honor to begin the final round of the GTE Classic, with Holtgrieve and Thompson following. "Luckily, we had enough volunteers around here to applaud as we introduced them," starter Gil Gonsalves said.

"When you're first off on Sunday, you'd probably rather be anywhere else than here, playing golf. They were very anxious to start. We had a minute to go and they were already telling me, 'Get us off the tee.' They were ready to go and run around the golf course, to get away from this week."

Barber began the day at 17-over-par 159. "When you play like I played (the first two rounds), you're going to be first off," he said. "It was nice this mornin', actually," Thompson said in his Plano, Texas, twang. "It ain't good bein' there, of course. I'm not sure I've ever done that in 10 years (actually 11 on the Senior PGA Tour)."

At 7:30, when the sun was low on the horizon, the moon was still in the sky and Bruce Fleisher was half an hour out of bed and having a cup of coffee, Gonsalves announced: "Ladies and gentlemen, from Sherman, Texas, Mr. Miller Barber." In deference to the respect for all the competitors, Gonsalves did it with the same stentorian voice he used more than four hours later to introduce Fleisher's threesome.

Leslie Williams, 57, of Syracuse applauded. So did Bill Gleeson, 68, of Punta Gorda. So did the four other spectators assembled … if that's the word … behind the green-and-white twine barrier surrounding the first tee. "With that many people," Williams said, "you have to clap louder."

"Six people," Barber said … he hadn't counted the house; it was just a guess. "That's just part of this game, just the way it is. If you play that poorly and you're first off and it's going to be that early in the morning, people aren't going to come out to watch you. But we had a few following us after the first seven or eight holes. I guess they wanted to see who was first off, and there we were."

Williams, seated to the right of the starter's tent and next to the crutches he is using while rehabilitating from hip surgery, arrived shortly before Barber and his playing partners. "I like to be right behind them so I can see the shot," he said. "This is the best seat and you've got to be here early to get it."

Gleeson stood about 20 feet to Williams' right, next to the green pole topped by the white board with the red No. 1 at the players' entrance to the tee. "This is the best spot. This is my spot," he said, as if he would have had to jostle someone for it.

Gleeson had been there since 6:30 … not just Sunday but each day of the tournament … when it was still kind of dark, "when you could see the full moon."

Bob Duval, part of the second threesome, was on the practice tee about that time. He looked up and saw the moon, looked back and saw the illuminated Outback sign against the lightening sky and said to his caddie, "This is not good."

Thompson was third to tee off. He had bogeyed, then birdied No. 1 the first two days. This time he made par. Barber birdied it; Holtgrieve bogeyed it. Without having to wait for anyone to hole out on the No. 2 green, they strolled toward the second tee.

"It's wonderful. Really. That's the great thing about it. You've got clear sailing," said Thompson, who won the tournament in 1994 and hasn't won a senior event since. "You work on your swing. You try to figure out why you're here so early, why you're playing so bad. You have 18 holes to figure it out. It's try this, try that. It's an experimental thing when you get to that point. You could shoot 66 and still wouldn't win but a couple of thousand bucks."

About four hours later, Barber, 68, winner of 11 PGA Tour events, of 24 senior tournaments, walked up the slope to the green at No. 18. He received cordial applause from the several hundred spectators beginning to fill the stadium seats. He made par to finish 24 over.

"I just played terrible this week. My timing wasn't there. My concentration wasn't there. Nothing was there. And it's all my fault. You have those kinds of weeks and you have to take the bad with the good."

At 11:40 a.m., Dana Quigley, five strokes back, began his ultimately futile final-round pursuit of Fleisher. Buses still were delivering spectators to the course and had not begun shuttling them back to their parked cars.

Barber already had signed his card with 7-over 78. He was sampling the soup in the clubhouse grille.

(February 21, 2000)

~ *Miller Barber's three-round total, a tournament-worst 24 over par, was 237. He earned $650. Rocky Thompson (230) was next-to-last and won $702. Jim Holtgrieve, one of three golfers at 228, earned $858. Bruce Fleisher won $195,000 with a final-round 2-under 69 finishing at 13-under 200, four strokes ahead of Dana Quigley.* ~

Thirty

Hatcher's style helps L.A. roll into Series

LOS ANGELES - Put a squirrel cage in the Dodgers' dugout with one of those endless wheels. Give Mickey Hatcher a place of his own, a way to run and run and run and not get in everybody's way.

"I can't help it," he says. "I just can't sit still. I'd go nuts."

He's already halfway there, jumping around, snorting, cheerleading, high-fiving everyone in sight. And prowling the dugout. Back and forth, back and forth, a caged tiger.

"My biggest problem," he says, "is all the guys yelling at me to sit my ass down so they can see the game."

Hatcher plays the game with all the grace of a five-car pileup on the Hollywood Freeway. His uniform gets filthy on the way to the on-deck circle. He runs back to the dugout faster after popping out than most guys do legging out a double.

"Infectious," manager Tommy Lasorda says. Virulent is more like it - a critical case of baseball fever.

"I have a nickname," he says. "They call me 'Looney Tunes.'"

He's the kind of guy no team can afford to be without, a big reason why the Dodgers are in the World Series.

Hatcher, statistically a hanger-on at best, keeps teammates loose and aroused. Don't dare let down or look down while Mickey's around.

"That's when I move in for the kill," he says. "If I see a young guy on the bench, down on himself, I let him know how terrible he is, how they're going to send him back down to the minor leagues tomorrow."

That's a joke, son.

"I try to get him loosened up. I remember those days. I've had enough of them. When you're going bad, nobody talks to you. I can't let a guy die like that, can't let him feel like he's the reason we lost."

He's a lot like Ray Knight, the catalyst of the 1986 Mets who won the World Series. Getting rid of Knight was like disconnecting their life-support system.

Hatcher's full-bore approach to the game is as involuntary a reflex as a liberal's knee-jerk, the result of years of football, in high school, at Mesa (Ariz.) Junior College and, for one year, at Oklahoma.

"In football, you can psych yourself up like crazy. If I stare at a wall long enough, I can convince myself I can run into it and it won't hurt me. Being a wide receiver, getting clotheslined and blind-sided, you can get yourself ready for anything."

Until this year, Hatcher was a victim of the worst kind of timing.

He made it to the Dodgers in 1979, the year after they played the Yankees in the World Series. At the start of 1981, the year L.A. beat the Yanks in the Series, he was traded to Minnesota. And at the start of 1987, the year the Twins won the Series, he was released.

Enough to drive anyone crazy.

"They thought I was going to tear up the locker room and start strangling people. But I knew it was my turn. All I told 'em was, 'Leave me a couple of tickets for the Series.' I just knew that team was going."

He was back home just outside Phoenix on April 10. Up by 6 every morning, unable to sleep. The 1987 season had started without him. Nobody was interested in him. He would run two miles each morning, then pick up the Arizona Republic from his neighbor's driveway, sit on his neighbor's porch and read the sports pages.

"One day I read how the Dodgers are 0-5 and (Bill) Madlock's hurt," Hatcher said. "I called Willie (Sanchez, his agent). He was talking about me to Oakland's farm team, Tacoma. 'Do me a favor,' I said, 'Call the Dodgers, ask if I can go to Triple-A ball for two weeks at my own expense.'

"Four hours later Willie calls back and says, 'How's it feel to be a Dodger?' I said, 'Great. I'll be in Albuquerque in an hour.' He said, 'They don't want you in Albuquerque. They want you in L.A.'"

This may be the last year they want him. The Jack Clark trade talk already has begun and if the Dodgers get him from the Yanks, what do they need with Hatcher, a guy who'll hit maybe .250 with five homers and 25 RBI? Inspiration? They've got Kirk Gibson.

"This World Series is the greatest thrill of my life," Hatcher said. "I'm going to hold onto this feeling as long as I can. It took nine years to get it, and you never know if it'll come around again."

When the end comes, he says, "I'll tell my wife to get a job and me and the kids'll hang around the golf course. I'll be a Mr. Mom. Maybe then I can stop running."

Fat chance.

(October 15, 1988)

⁓ In the first inning of Game 1 of the World Series against Oakland on Oct. 15, Mickey Hatcher hit a home run, matching his total for the entire

1988 season. Kirk Gibson's ninth-inning home run off Dennis Eckersley won the game. The Dodgers won the World Series in five games, during which Hatcher batted .368 (7-for 19), leading the team with two home runs, five runs batted in and five runs scored. It was his only World Series. Hatcher spent the 1989-90 seasons with the Dodgers and 1991 with their Triple-A minor-league team in Albuquerque, then retired and became a coach and minor-league manager. ⌁

Thirty-one

Seeing Wrigley in a New Light

An era goes gentle into that good night tonight

CHICAGO - It's no big deal, really. Just the end of an era. Like Fenway up in Boston, Wrigley Field will be just another place to play baseball, to get going by the seventh inning because the game's dragging and it's getting chilly and the kids are cranky.

You won't even be able to see the stanchions, the latticework frames and the six banks of lights atop the leftfield and rightfield stands if you're looking out toward centerfield from behind home plate.

It'll look pretty much the same, just another Phillies-Cubs game tonight, a couple of second-division teams playing out the schedule.

Except it'll look, well, different.

It'll be dark above, and along, Waveland and Sheffield beyond the ivy-walled bleachers.

There'll be more competition for the parking spaces as the working residents of Wrigleyville return home, arriving along with the Cubs' fans motoring in from the South Side and the suburbs.

"It doesn't feel like the end of an era," said Ernie Banks, Mr. Cub, who played 2,528 games in his 19 seasons, who never came even remotely close to a World Series, who hit 290 of his 512 career home runs at Wrigley.

"When I first came into the majors, nobody ever believed the Dodgers or the Giants would go to California, or that Jackie Robinson would play in the big leagues. But they did," Banks said.

"And in my advanced years, I've learned that change is a big part of life, and that baseball has learned to deal with it much better than almost any other part of our society.

"Wrigley Field is still there, after all, and it's still one of the most beautiful spots on this Earth. The only difference," Banks said, "is now we have lights."

Oh, the great monoliths of television and the Tribune Co. will abide by the decree for a time. Seven night games this season, 18 for each of the next 14 seasons. By then, enough people will probably have forgotten what all the fuss was about and in the year 2003, if (when) the Cubs are in their 58th season without a World Series at its end, there will be more night games, maybe half a season's worth.

Or maybe Wrigley Field will by then have outlived its usefulness and the Cubs will be playing in some dome-ceilinged, artificial-turfed stadium, and some northsiders will be living in Wrigley Field apartments or shopping at the Wrigley Mall at 1060 West Addison St. For now, though, games will still be played here.

"If you want to preserve what's best of the past, you have to change," National League president Bart Giamatti said July 25, when the lights were turned on here for the first time. "And the best way to preserve day baseball and this lovely, wonderful ballpark, is to play a few night games."

In the heart of old Chicago,
Round Addison and Clark,
Is a windy, sunny, ivy-covered
Legend of a park
Where the fans are just as famous
As the men who come to play,

210

In fabled Wrigley Field
Where the stars come out by day.

When the Tribune Co., owner of the Chicago Tribune and cable superstation WGN (which televises Cubs games nationwide), bought the team in August 1981 for $20.5-million, it began campaigning to bring Wrigley Field into line with the 25 other major-league teams, to add the last link to the chain that began May 24, 1935, in Cincinnati, a chain that had been dangling since Briggs Stadium installed lights on June 15, 1948. The Detroit Tigers thus became the last of the original 16 teams to add lights.

In October 1981, Dallas Green arrived as the Cubs' general manager and spearheaded the drive for night games.

"I'd been born and raised in night baseball. It was all I'd ever known," Green said from suburban Philadelphia, where he lives on a 60-acre farm in a 200-year-old farmhouse.

"But after I'd been at Wrigley for two or three years, I began to get a feel for what baseball was like in the daytime. I started to get some second thoughts about whether night games were really all that necessary. They drew 2-million or so each year, the place had a great family atmosphere. After a while I didn't know what all the fighting was about, why we absolutely had to have lights, other than to satisfy the ownership of the other clubs, the commitments they'd made for national TV and so on."

So Green has "come 180 degrees," he said - this same man who had suggested in 1985 that the Cubs, if they ever again made it into the playoffs (as they had in 1984), might have to play their post-season games elsewhere - St. Louis, for example.

Of course, he is also the man who helped put together much of the current Cubs team, then resigned under less-than-amicable circumstances a few weeks after the 1987 season.

"I think baseball's missing a great deal by not allowing the Cubs that singular honor of being the only baseball team in the only park in the majors not to have lights," Green said. "I just think baseball and TV are forgetting that this is - was - something special."

Hack Wilson took the field here,
And took the ball downtown,
And Beckert scooped 'em up here,
And Jenkins gunned 'em down,
And Williams hit to Waveland,
And Brickhouse said, "Hey, Hey!"
In Wrigley Field, Chicago,
Where the stars come out by day.

It was supposed to be that way for all time. That's what Phillip K. Wrigley promised.

But nothing is forever, any more than the 23rd Street Grounds were, or Lakefront Park was, or West Side Park was or the West Side Grounds were, when Chicago was playing National League Baseball during 1876-1915. This wasn't even the Cubs' home when it opened in 1914.

Then, again, it wasn't even Wrigley Field then. It was Weeghman Park, home of restaurateur Charles H. Weeghman's Chicago Whales in the short-lived Federal League. Then it was Cubs Park, when the National Leaguers moved in in 1916 and christened the place with an 11-inning, 7-6 victory over Cincinnati - with a live bear cub in attendance.

It wasn't until 1926 that William Wrigley Jr., the chewing-gum magnate and owner of the team, put his name on its home.

It wasn't until 1938 that Bill Veeck, then a Cubs executive (and later maverick owner of the White Sox), planted the Bittersweet ivy along the outfield walls.

It was here, on Sept. 26, 1908, that Ed Reulbach of the Cubs pitched both games of a doubleheader against Brooklyn, shutting out the Dodgers 5-0 and 3-0.

It was here, on May 2, 1917, that the Reds' Fred Toney and the Cubs' Hippo Vaughn each pitched nine innings of hitless ball before Cincinnati broke through with a couple of 10th-inning hits and won 1-0.

It was here, in the 1932 World Series, that Babe Ruth of the Yankees supposedly reacted to the taunts of the Cubs by pointing to the flagpole in centerfield and hitting Charlie Root's next pitch to the very spot.

It was here, on Sept. 28, 1938, that Gabby Hartnett hit the "Homer in the Gloamin'," a two-out shot into the encroaching darkness in the bottom of the ninth off Mace Brown of Pittsburgh, a shot that helped propel the Cubs to a pennant.

It was here, on May 12, 1970, that Ernie Banks hit his 500th career home run, and here on Aug. 22, 1982, that Banks had his uniform number (14) retired.

It is here, on Aug. 8, 1988, that Rick Sutcliffe of the Cubs will throw a baseball under artificial light.

"There's always going to be another World Series, always going to be another All-Star Game," Sutcliffe said. "But there's only one opening night."

There have been other night-time events here - professional wrestling, boxing, a rodeo, even a Harlem Globetrotters basketball game.

But never baseball. William Wrigley Jr. died three years before lights came to the majors. The club passed to his son, Philip, who vowed that lights would never shine upon the ballpark.

Philip died in 1977 and the club passed to his son, William.

Five years later, William sold it and the battle began - the Tribune Co. on one side, tradition, nostalgia, the neighborhood and Citizens United for Baseball in the Sunshine (CUBS) on the other.

"For seven years, we won every battle against one of the most powerful corporations around," said CUBS member Mike Quigley. "We won in the City Council, in the (state) legislature and on every referendum   that was held. But they only had to win once."

In 1982, the state enacted a noise-pollution statute so specifically worded that night games were permitted in the neighborhoods encompassing Comiskey Park, the White Sox's home, and Soldier Field, where the NFL's Chicago Bears play - but prohibiting them where Wrigley Field stands. In 1983 the city enacted similar legislation.

But as the team began threatening to move out of Wrigley Field, and   as Chicago aldermen began thinking about the Cubs' $100-million or more economic impact on the city, sentiment began to shift. Last February, the City Council approved the legislation that lifted the ban on night games. Not so coincidentally, Major League Baseball announced that   Wrigley Field would be the site of the 1990 All-Star Game.

The anti-lights forces haven't given up. Because the state's noise-pollution statute remains on the books (if unenforced), CUBS says it plans to monitor decibel levels at night games, and is considering a   November referendum that would seek to ban the sale of alcoholic beverages (beer) in the ward encompassing Wrigley Field.

"You tell me that a last-place ballclub that sold 2.4-million tickets last year (turnstile count: 2,035,130) needs additional revenue," said CUBS' Quigley, "and I'm reminded of what P. K. Wrigley said when they told him to put in lights in the late 1960s: 'It's not   night baseball we need. It's winning baseball.'"

And Mr. Cub, he wowed 'em,
And so did Mr. Veeck,
And Harry Holy Cow'd 'em,
And Leo gave 'em heck,
And Ryno rocked the rooftops,
And Dawson made 'em sway.
In righteous Wrigley Field,
Where the stars come out by day.

As night games become a reality, the Cubs' critics will have to find another reason for the team's failures. No longer will they be able to point to the long, hot summers under the sun and claim that September swoons are a byproduct of free-flowing sweat, that the players wilted along with the ivy, as reasons why the Cubs haven't been in a World Series since 1945 and haven't won one since 1908.

"When I pitch a night game," said Sutcliffe, tonight's starter against Philadelphia, "I lose about three pounds. But during a day game at Wrigley, I lose anywhere from six to 10 pounds. It's tougher for your body to come back from that."

And despite the obvious night-time diversions that ballplayers (Cubs and visiting teams) can enjoy after an afternoon at Wrigley Field, the home team professes delight that the schedule is changing for the darker.

"If you asked the guys, more than half of them would prefer to play night games instead of day games," said pitcher Greg Maddux.

Lee Elia, the Phillies' manager, says it's nice to be a part of history. "I've always been extremely proud to say I was a member of the Chicago Cubs," he said. "And now to be a part of a historical ballgame even makes it more special."

This is the same Lee Elia, it must be noted, who, one day, lit into the self-proclaimed Bleacher Bums and the rest of the Cubs fans who, during his brief managerial reign in Chicago during 1982-83, packed the ballpark and vented their frustrations at the fifth-place finishers.

The fans would do better, Elia said in an expletive-sprinkled outburst, to "go out and get a job and find out what it's like to make a living. Eighty percent of the world's out making a living. The other 15 come out here." They will still come, of course, particularly tonight against the Phillies and tomorrow night against the Mets (the third of this year's seven night games is scheduled for Monday, Aug. 22, against Houston).

They, too, will be sellouts.

Five weeks ago, when the remaining 13,000 available seats for tonight's game went on sale, more than 1.5-million phone calls to the Cubs were attempted. It was, Illinois Bell said, the busiest day in Chicago phone history.

"It'll be a zoo," longtime Bleacher Bum Elsie Foydl told The Associated Press. "We've lost tradition and that's a little sad." She said she wouldn't be at the game. "Much of what we held dear is gone," she said. "It's a business, you know."

But another fan, Jerry Pritikin, looked on the brighter side of night ball. "It's going to be magnificent to look at the bleachers under lights," he said. "The ivy will be effervescent."

So sing it from the boxes
And shout it from the bleachers,
Of a celebrated past,
And the brightest of all futures.
And won't it be a party,
And won't it be a sight,
When finally, at Wrigley,
The stars come out at night.

- Poem by Craig Constantine, creative services producer, WGN-TV.

(August 8, 1988)

~ *The Cubs were leading the Phillies 3-1 in the bottom of the fourth inning when rain halted play. After waiting 129 minutes, the game was rained out. On August 9, the following night, the Cubs defeated the Mets 6-4 in Wrigley Field's first official night game. The Cubs played 30 night games at Wrigley Field in 2013 and 38 in 2014. They still haven't been in a World Series since 1945.* ~

Thirty-two

Math on the high seas... go figure

It has come to our attention, here in the Department of Really Useless Nautical Information, that a vast majority of the reading sporting public has no idea what 42 meters means.

The chief petty officer here in the department's Offshore Division advises that "42 meters" is a copyrighted expression tossed around with aggravating regularity by the hoity-toity America's Cup crowd.

(Hoity-toity is a technical naval phrase meaning, "How do you like my cashmere blue blazer and pure silk cravat, and how can we be out of champagne when it's only noon?")

Forty-two meters refers, of course, to the size of each America's Cup boat being sailed off the coast of San Diego on a 20-mile course conforming to the lower digestive tract of an arachnid (hence the term "eight legs").

Excuse me. The rear admiral (and we mean that in the kindest possible sense) of the division's Keelhaul Subsection advises us that what is sailing off the coast of San Diego is not boats but yachts.

The technical difference between a boat and a yacht is that our friends who spend money on lawn service and kennels and still have a lot left over, they own boats, but even they aren't rich enough to own a yacht (and that blue blazer-and-cravat routine on the 12-footer in their driveway is getting awfully old).

Okay, so they're yachts.

They're 42-meter yachts.

But why 42 meters?

We measured a few of these bo- these yachts (*fine!*) when Dennis Conner wasn't looking, and we discovered that they're not 42 meters long.

Or high. Or deep. Or across. Or around. Or anything else.

When Dennis turned around, we asked him which part of his boat was 42 meters (we figured maybe it had something to do with the engine), but all he did was start yelling things like "Hoist the scupper!" and "Trim the mizzenmast!" and "It's a yacht! *A yacht!*"

We tried to ask a few of the other yachtspeople, but we were drowned out by the sound of pure silk being compared to cashmere. Then we found an algebraic equation scribbled on a cocktail napkin:

Length plus 1.25 times the square root of the sail area minus 9.8 times the cube root of displacement divided by 0.388 could equal no more than 42 meters.

We had stumbled upon the secret. It was so obvious that even a child of 10 with a degree in astrophysics could figure it out.

Yeah, well, we knew most of that all along. The longer the bo-yacht, the faster it goes. The more sail it has, the faster it goes. The heavier it is, the slower it goes. And that 1.25 and 9.8 business, well, those are just, umm, numbers to balance the system. Sort of like the way the NFL says a quarterback has to complete 70 percent of his passes to offset 1½ interceptions or something.

But that 0.388. Why did we have to divide everything by that? Our department's resident 10-year-old couldn't figure it out. Her degree is in *theoretical* physics. Like, duh.

If it hadn't been for John Marshall, we might never have found out.

Marshall was on the committee to establish the new America's Cup rules. Now he runs the Partnership for America's Cup Technology (PACT) in Addison, Maine. He also doesn't own a yacht.

We called and asked him about that 0.388.

"It's a joke," he said.

We threatened to pour champagne all over his blue blazer and cravat.

"No, really," Marshall insisted. "There's this cult science-fiction book, *The Hitch-Hiker's Guide to the Galaxy*. It poses a series of cosmic questions, like, 'What is the meaning of life?' and so on.

"When you get to the end of the book, the answer to every important question is 42. So when we sat down to create the America's Cup yacht, we decided that the number, after all the adding and subtracting and multiplying and dividing, should be 42. We worked backwards - and 0.388 was the number that everything had to be divided by to get to 42."

He was not making it up. Really.

Well, we in the Yawl Subdivision (a southern naval term) of the Department of Really Useless Nautical Information applaud the America's Cup crowd for its rollicking good humor.

We can only hope that the price of pure silk and cashmere go through the roof some day so all those hoity-toity *yacht*people will be reduced to drinking beer and trying to back their *boat* into their driveway.

(April 15, 1992)

Thirty-three

Mets rekindle magic feeling, but then get back to the future

NEW YORK - The beauty of sport is that time stands still and moves on simultaneously.

Names come and go, but the game remains. Ed Delahanty played it 99 years ago. Cy Young and Babe Ruth and Josh Gibson and Ted Williams and Sandy Koufax and Roy Campanella played it.

Last Oct. 27, Rich Gedman played it here.

When the Shea Stadium press box was unlocked Tuesday, the blackboard read:

Boston	Mets
Boggs 3b	Wilson cf
Barrett 2b	Teufel 2b
Buckner 1b	Hernandez 1b
Rice lf	Carter c
Evans rf	Strawberry rf
Gedman c	Knight 3b
Henderson cf	Mitchell lf
Owen ss	Santana ss
Hurst p	Darling p

Time had stood still here. Jesse Orosco's glove still hadn't fallen back to earth. The Mets' laughter still hadn't faded; Red Sox tears still streamed. There had been no off-season, no spring training, no failed drug tests, no trades.

But, of course, there had been.

Gedman was in that limbo of free agency, shunned by the rest of the American League, unable to return to the Red Sox.

Ray Knight, a hero when the lights went out here barely five months   ago, had exiled himself to Baltimore. Kevin Mitchell had been sacrificed to San Diego.

Suddenly, a wet rag obliterated the names. Time no longer stood still here. "Pittsburg," the blackboard read moments later, the club-house attendant having dropped the h.

Bonds cf …

Rachel Robinson stood beside second base, a black No. 42 printed on it. Her husband, Jackie, once played baseball in Brooklyn. A few of his teammates tried to force the Dodgers to keep him off the club. They failed.

In 1947, Dixie Walker had been the ringleader of the loyal opposition to anyone who wasn't white. Walker's nickname was, in that Brooklynesque way of talking, "The People's Cherce." In 1948, Walker was gone.

Because of Jackie Robinson, Darryl Strawberry had a chance to play baseball for the New York Mets on Tuesday.

Robinson's name received polite applause, a few cheers, during the pregame ceremonies.

The cheers could never be loud enough, long enough. But time passes and people forget.

They introduced the Pittsburgh Pirates. It was like putting a lounge act on ahead of Sinatra. They received the "Yeah, okay, right" kind of applause from the 46,102 paying customers who couldn't have cared less about guys named Bream and Bonilla and Belliard.

Then they introduced the Mets who weren't here a year ago. Kevin McReynolds, who came east when Mitchell headed west, received an ovation. He was clearly surprised. He doffed his cap. He got another, louder ovation. He turned to a teammate and giggled.

Then they handed out the World Series rings. No. 19, Bob Ojeda, got his first. He had work to do. He would be pitching for the Mets. He had to warm up.

After that, they emerged in numerical order. No. 1, Mookie Wilson. No. 3, Rafael Santana. No. 4, Lenny Dykstra, and so on. Handshakes all around from National League president A. Bartlett Giamatti, Mets chairman Nelson Doubleday, president Fred Wilpon, and general manager Frank Cashen.

No. 11, Tim Teufel. No. 12, Ron Darling …

One by one, they ran up to home plate to receive their rings. They had the childlike smiles of Little Leaguers getting their free post-game sodas.

No. 15, Rick Aguilera. No. 17, Keith Hernandez. No. 18, Darryl Strawberry …

No mention of No. 16. On Tuesday, Dwight Gooden was a nonperson.

Dave Magadan was there. He's on injured reserve, recovering from surgery. Roger McDowell was there. He's on IR, recovering from surgery. Gooden wasn't there. Neither was his picture, his name. Nothing. No banners took note of his absence.

"We didn't want to get maudlin," Cashen said later.

While the crowd was assembling, about half an hour before the ceremonies started, the DiamondVision screen above the leftfield fence showed highlights of the World Series.

In slow-motion and stop-action, the ball bounced through Bill Buckner's legs. The fans cheered.

Then, during the ceremonies, as Cashen and manager Davey Johnson carried the World Series Champions banner out to a color guard, the film was shown again.

In slow-motion and stop-action, the ball bounced through Bill Buckner's legs again. The fans roared.

Orosco threw the ball. Threw his glove. Cut to the World Series trophy. Cut to the ticker-tape parade, a uniquely New York tradition.

Glenn Close sang the National Anthem. Halfway through, the fans began their throaty "let's-get-on-with-it" cheer, another New York tradition.

Some traditions are better than others.

A few minutes later, Ojeda pumped and threw a pitch to Barry Bonds.

The Mets were no longer champions. They were defending champions, and 1986 no longer counted.

In 1980, when the Mets were still a team to be pitied, they stretched a slogan across the portals of Shea Stadium. "The Magic is Back!" it proclaimed.

They finished fifth that year.

In 1981 the slogan was changed to "The Magic is Real!"

They finished fifth again.

For a couple of years they abstained, and wound up sixth - last - each time.

In 1984, with Strawberry in his second season and Gooden in his first, the Mets tried again, this time with the suggestion: "Catch the Rising Stars!"

They finished second to Chicago. They stuck with it in '85 and finished second.

In 1986 the slogan was: "Baseball Like It Oughta Be!"

And they won it all.

This year, a simple statement: "1986 World Champs!" Nice and clean. No pretense.

They'll either have to change one number next year - or come up with an explanation.

(April 8, 1987)

∽ Darryl Strawberry hit a three-run homer in the first inning. The Mets won 3-2. Rich Gedman returned to the Red Sox in 1987 and was traded to Houston in 1990. Dwight Gooden tested positive for cocaine in the spring of 1987, entered a rehabilitation program April 1 and did not pitch until June 5. In 1987 the Mets finished second. They didn't return to the World Series until 2000, when they lost to the Yankees in five games. They reached the World Series again in 2015 and lost to the Kansas City Royals, also in five games. ∽

Thirty-four

Tales of wins and nagging failures

His name was Silky Sullivan and oh, my, could he run.

He was a handsome beast, as muscular as a quarterhorse, his scarlet coat glinting like burnished bronze. And his cavalry charges made him the people's choice.

He would give away half the backstretch, then turn on the speed and make up unbelievable chunks of ground with each stride. And win. That's how he won the Santa Anita Derby. From 30 lengths back.

But that was California. This was Louisville, Ky. This was Churchill Downs.

This was 1958, the 84th running of the Kentucky Derby. Silky Sullivan went off as the second favorite. If he could win this 1¼-mile first jewel in thoroughbred racing's Triple Crown, he would carry Bill Shoemaker to his second Derby win in four years.

Silky Sullivan left the gate from the 12th post position and, in a few strides, was his accustomed last. At the half-mile pole, he was 11 lengths behind the next-to-last horse.

At the turn, he turned it on, and under a gun-metal sky a roar emerged from the throats of thousands of spectators who had come to see if this magnificent animal was more than a West Coast wonder.

229

He wasn't. Tim Tam wore the garland of roses and paid $4.20 for a $2 win ticket, the same as Silky Sullivan would have paid.

As quickly as Silky Sullivan's charge had begun it had ended, and with it his mystique. He finished where he began, 12th. He may have been a wonderful horse, but he wasn't great.

An ego and a wallet to match

There was a time when just about any horseman with a big enough ego and wallet to match could put a thoroughbred in the Kentucky Derby. The current price is $20,600 just to get in - $600 to nominate the horse, $10,000 to enter and another $10,000 to start the race.

The 100th running, in 1974, had a 23-horse stampede. These days the field is limited to 20. If more than that enter, the field is decided on career earnings from stakes races.

There have been many great 3-year-olds who, on the first Saturday in May, have won the Run for the Roses - Gallant Fox and War Admiral, Whirlaway and Citation, Secretariat and Spectacular Bid. In all, 47 of the 116 post-time favorites have won.

But the Kentucky Derby has never been a race just for favorites. Long-shot winners abound, like Donerail (92-1 in 1913), Gallahadion (35-1 in 1940) and, more recently, Ferdinand (18-1 in 1986).

But there are long shots and then there are …

Eddie Anderson (Rochester on the Jack Benny program) owned Burnt Cork, a horse of no particular note. But in 1943, Anderson wanted to be part of the Derby crowd. Count Fleet won the race. Burnt Cork stopped trying halfway through the race and finished last, eight lengths behind the ninth-place finisher.

In 1979 it was Great Redeemer, a maiden (a horse who has never won a race). He had never finished within 10 lengths of the winner in any of his seven career starts. This was even worse. Great Redeemer, 79-1 at post time, was 25 lengths away from next-to-last and 48 back of the winner, Spectacular Bid.

In 1975, Bombay Duck went off at 28-1. He set the pace for the first half of the race but heading down the backstretch he suddenly quit, finishing last (15th), 35 lengths back of winner Foolish Pleasure. Rumors that Bombay Duck had been hit by a beer can thrown by one of the more rowdy infield spectators were fueled by a grapefruit-sized welt the horse had when he got back to his stall.

The only one-eyed starter

This year's extra long-shot entries include Big Al's Express and Wilder Than Ever.

Big Al's Express arrived from Vallejo, Calif., in a one-horse trailer pulled by a truck driven by his co-owner and trainer, Thomas Allen. Big Al's Express had not only never won a race; until Saturday's Derby Trial the colt had never run a race.

And he got into that race only after he took a test to see if he could handle a starting gate. The first time, he didn't. Last Wednesday, Big Al's Express sat down in the gate. It took three guys to get him out. On Thursday and Friday, he passed.

He didn't do much passing Saturday. He finished last in the Trial and was treated for exhaustion. He finished about 31 lengths behind the winner, Alydavid, after bumping Alydavid at the start.

Wilder Than Ever is a non-winner in six starts this year, although he did finish third in the Jim Beam Stakes after going off at 118-1.

Raymond Cottrell Sr. owns Wilder Than Ever. He also owns Fighting Fantasy, whom he entered in last year's Kentucky Derby as a favor to his 6-year-old granddaughter, Ashley, who was in the hospital. Fighting Fantasy led after a quarter-mile. He finished last, 49 lengths behind Unbridled, the winner.

Then there was 1982 entry Cassaleria, the only recorded one-eyed starter in the 116 years of the Kentucky Derby. (There may have been others - one-eyed horses are not all that rare - but none officially was registered as such at Churchill Downs.)

Cassaleria, racing under the silks of the appropriately named 20/20 Stable, had lost his left eye within hours of birth when he fell against his stall wall while trying to stand up.

He ran well, if not winningly, in California stakes races.

Cassaleria's owner, Tom Gentry, was publicity-mad, hiring a plane to fly over the track to promote the claustrophobic colt, distributing balloons all over Louisville and so on. It didn't help. (It didn't hurt, either.) Cassaleria went off at 26-1 and finished 13th.

At least Cassaleria got in the Derby. Twenty years earlier, when the appropriately named One Eyed Tom arrived in Louisville, track stewards insisted he show he could handle a starting gate. Wise request. When he came out of the gate, One Eyed Tom made a left turn that could have wiped out half the field. His entry was rejected.

Remember Jacklin Klugman? That horse, like Burnt Cork, was owned by an actor. But Jack Klugman's horse was no rank outsider, having won seven of 10 starts including the California Derby. What made Jacklin Klugman so interesting was that everyone thought he was a filly. He wasn't. He also didn't win, finishing third behind Genuine Risk.

(April 28, 1991)

⌖ Strike The Gold won the 117th running of the Kentucky Derby. Wilder Than Ever finished 15th, next to last. Big Al's Express never made it to the starting gate. Not on race day, that is. He sat down in it during a workout three days earlier and was pulled from the field. ⌖

Thirty-five

Fallen hero looms over Colorado's rise

B OULDER, Colo. - *"Don't be saddened that you no longer see me in the flesh because I assure you I will always be with you in spirit. Hold me dear to your hearts as you know I do all of you. Strive only for victory each time we play and trust in the Lord, for He truly is the way. I love you all. Go get 'em, and bring home the Orange Bowl."* - **Sal Aunese, who died Sept. 23, 1989.**

For two years, Sal Aunese was the starting quarterback at the University of Colorado, and little more. He was a sociology major whose impact on campus and on the Buffaloes' football program would have ended with his graduation.

He was born in the San Diego suburb of Oceanside. His Samoan parents named him Siasau Pepa Aunese. He was a marginal student at Colorado, forced to sit out the 1986 season, his first year of eligibility, after failing to meet the grade-point requirements of the NCAA's Proposition 48.

He was suspended from spring practice in 1988 and spent two weeks in jail that summer - part of a two-year deferred sentence - after pleading guilty to misdemeanor charges of assault, trespassing and menacing.

Aunese (a-NESS-ee) started seven games as a sophomore and all 11 plus the Freedom Bowl as a junior. The Buffaloes were 8-4 in 1988, and Aunese blamed himself for narrow losses to Big Eight powers Oklahoma and Nebraska. He hoped to lead Colorado this year to its first conference championship since 1976, its first perfect season since 1923 and its first national championship ever.

In March, he was diagnosed as having inoperable stomach cancer. At 8:47 p.m. on Saturday, Sept. 23, Sal Aunese died. He was 21.

He has become a legend, a cause. He has become more to this team in death than he was in life.

The players have left an empty seat on the plane, an unoccupied bed in a hotel room on the road. They have left a vacant place at their training table.

They have knelt on the field and pointed at the sky in silent tribute to Aunese before road and home games.

They wear his name on their left sleeves and paste labels of his No. 8 on their helmets, their shoulder pads, their towels - everywhere.

Colorado has preserved his locker, his possessions, in glass.

A wood carving at the entrance to the locker room celebrates Aunese as "a quarterback for life."

And the players often refer to him in the present tense.

Sal Aunese - an average quarterback in life, a typical young man with virtues and flaws like any other - pervades Colorado football.

And the Buffaloes - unbeaten, untied and ranked No. 1 going into their New Year's night game against Notre Dame in the Orange Bowl - are on the threshold of achieving those goals Aunese set.

"Sal had a real impact on us," Colorado coach Bill McCartney said. "He brought us together. Sal was team. That's the legacy he has left behind."

He has left behind more than a memory. There is his son, Timothy.

The mother is Kristyn McCartney, the coach's daughter. She gave birth last April 24, still lives at home and is raising him with her parents' help.

When the baby was born, it was understood that Sal was the father, but no one wrote that, or said it publicly - even during one preseason practice when Kristyn showed up with Timothy dressed in a miniature football jersey bearing Aunese's No. 8, even when Aunese cradled the baby in his arms.

"The first year he was here, '86, we were dating on and off since then," said Kristyn, who has temporarily withdrawn from school. "I was his girlfriend for a while, but when he found out about my pregnancy, he decided to call it off. He was afraid and he didn't know what to do and he thought the best thing was to ignore it. He kind of ran away."

They never discussed marriage as an option. "Neither of us wanted that," she said.

'But I have something no one ever had'

On Oct. 8, 1988, after the Oklahoma State game, Aunese met Cindy Shafer, another Colorado student and member of the university's sports information staff. They began dating.

"We were together almost every day," Shafer said. "We never thought about getting engaged or married. But I have something no one ever had. I had his love. I think (Kristyn) feels hurt because Sal wasn't with her. He was with me. She loved him but he didn't love her," Shafer said.

McCartney's voice quavered with emotion when she heard those words. "She makes it sound like it was a one-night stand," the coach's daughter said, "when it was so much more than that."

On Sept.25, two days after Aunese died, memorial services were conducted in the Old Main building on the Colorado campus. Aunese, in a suit and a lava-lava, a traditional calico skirt worn by South Sea islanders, lay in an open casket on the stark proscenium. His team-mates, coaches and members of the athletic department filed past to pay their respects.

Later, 2,000 people filled the auditorium. Kristyn McCartney, holding her 5-month-old son, and Cindy Shafer stood together. Aunese's parents, brothers and sisters, in Samoan tradition, draped the now-closed coffin with flowers and a hand-woven blanket and sang songs more festive than funereal.

Several players spoke at the memorial, as did clergy and Bill Mc-Cartney.

And in an emotional moment, the coach turned to his 19-year-old daughter and publicly acknowledged what almost everyone knew - that Aunese was the father of her child.

"You could have had an abortion," McCartney said. "You could have gone away and had the baby somewhere else to avoid the shame. But you didn't. You stayed and you're going to raise that little guy and all of us are going to have an opportunity to watch him. Kristyn, I admire you, I respect you and I love you so much."

Teammates refuse to let a memory fade. Aunese's futile fight against cancer elevated him to near sainthood among his teammates. They have turned their season into a crusade in his honor.

Arthur Walker, a senior defensive tackle from Houston, said the Buffaloes would have been as good with Aunese as they have been without him. But teammates aren't so sure.

"I think we've played a lot on emotion sometimes. We saw him struggle," said Darian Hagan, a sophomore from Los Angeles who succeeded Aunese at quarterback - and, some say, might have won the starting job from him this year.

"He made us want to do things that we didn't think we could do," Hagan said. "My season is for him. Everybody's is."

Jeff Campbell, a senior wide receiver from nearby Vail, repeatedly spoke of Aunese in the present tense. "He's still here," Campbell said. "He still goes with us. All of his stuff goes with us on trips.

"He hasn't missed a beat all year long. One of the things he never wanted us to do was let him go and we haven't let him go. He's the reason why this team is doing so well."

Aunese's death and the birth of his son are but the parts of the Colorado phenomenon that emerged from the ashes of McCartney's first three seasons here, a cumulative 7-25-1 record during 1982-84, including an injury-wracked 1-10 season that third year.

By the mid-1980s, McCartney's recruiting abilities had taken hold, but new problems had emerged - more than two dozen arrests for everything from petty mischief and trespassing to assault and rape.

Aunese's arrest followed his ransacking of a dormitory room after a fellow student yelled racist remarks at him, one of several racial incidents on campus and in town. This year, Boulder and university officials created a Community Task Force on Race Relations.

The tensions between the team and the community have been eased, on the surface at least, in the wake of Colorado's success and the Aunese saga that began in 1987 when, in the third game of the season, he came off the bench to replace injured starter Mark Hatcher.

Aunese rushed for 185 yards in barely three quarters. The next week, he was the starter for good.

As a junior last year he amassed the most total offense (1,401 yards) in a decade at Colorado. Even then, though, his former coach at Vista High School, Dick Haines, said it seemed as if Aunese looked different, perhaps a bit slower. And Dave Burton, Colorado's director of sports medicine, remembered Aunese complaining that he didn't feel quite right.

Last March, when Aunese reported for his physical prior to spring practice, he said he thought he had the flu. Preliminary tests at University Hospital in Denver revealed swollen glands. Then more tests.

The diagnosis: sarcoidosis, a lung disease, possibly pneumonia. Then a biopsy. That was when it was determined Aunese had stomach cancer and that the disease had spread to his lungs and lymph nodes near the lungs.

Three weeks later, Timothy McCartney was born.

'He chose to stay . . . I know I wouldn't'

Adeno carcinoma of the stomach is a rare form of cancer in this country – the American Cancer Society says it is more prevalent among Asians - and surgery, the usual treatment for stomach cancer, is ineffective since there are often no symptoms of the disease until the tumors have begun to spread.

Aunese began undergoing chemotherapy.

He made his first public appearance after the diagnosis when he attended the varsity-alumni spring game on April 28. When Hagan threw a long touchdown pass, he turned to Aunese and saluted him. Aunese stood and cheered his teammates. At the end, they carried their stricken quarterback off the field.

On May 8, 1989, Aunese's 21st birthday, Boulder County Court Judge Thomas Reed terminated the remaining year of his deferred sentence.

On Aug. 14, the first day of fall practice, Aunese was driven onto Folsom Field. He tried to speak but was on the verge of tears. Go back to work, he told them. They did, finishing the practice with a prayer for him. They did so after every practice.

When his teammates defeated visiting Illinois 38-7 on Sept.16, Aunese, on oxygen support, watched from a private box at Folsom Field.

He vowed then, as he had before, that he would accompany the Buffaloes to their Oct. 28 game at Oklahoma. He wanted to be there, he said, to see them avenge their 17-14 loss a year earlier to the Sooners, one for which he blamed himself.

On Sept.23, he died.

The following Saturday, Sept. 30, at Washington's Husky Stadium in Seattle, 60 Colorado players knelt on the turf, bowed their heads and pointed toward the sky in a silent farewell.

"Sal had a character, a spirit about him," senior linebacker Michael Jones said. "When he was sick, he had a chance to go back home. I know San Diego has a great facility for cancer patients. But he chose to stay here. That showed a lot about him. I don't know how many guys would stay. I know I wouldn't. I'd want to be home with my family."

But the team had meant as much to Aunese as he did to it. "He was the one person who was close to everyone on the team," Cindy Shafer said.

Shortly before Aunese died, he wrote a letter to his teammates which said, in part: "Don't be saddened that you no longer see me in the flesh because I assure you I will always be with you in spirit. Hold me dear to your hearts as you know I do all of you. Strive only for victory each time we play and trust in the Lord, for He truly is the way. I love you all. Go get 'em, and bring home the Orange Bowl."

A version of the letter is etched on a 300-pound, 4-by-5-foot oak carving by a local wildlife artist, a tribute to Aunese that adorns the entrance to the locker room. It depicts defensive tackle Okland Salavea, another Samoan and Aunese's closest friend on the team, kneeling in his No. 99 uniform and pointing to the Colorado sky with the Rocky Mountains in the background.

To the right of the carving and down the aisle is Aunese's locker.

Except for the glass panes, its neat appearance - his gold helmet, black-and-gold uniform and black cleats in place, the photograph of him being carried off the field at that spring game, and several poems engraved on plaques - it doesn't look all that different from the others.

One of the poems, by Edgar Guest, reads:

When I come to the end of the road,
And the sun has set for me,
I want no rites in a gloom-filled room.
Why cry for a soul set free?
Miss me a little but not too long,
And not with your head bowed low.
Remember the love that we once shared.
Miss me but let me go.
For this is a journey that we all must take,
And each must go alone.
It's all a part of the Master's plan,
A step on the road to home.
When you are lonely and sick at heart,
Go to the friends we know,
And bury your sorrows in doing good deeds.
Miss me but let me go.

They haven't let him go, from the empty seat on the plane, the kneeling on the field and pointing toward the sky and the rest of the spiritual trappings.

Criticism of the 'secular canonization'

There has been criticism from media and competing schools that the Buffaloes, in their consecration of Aunese, have exceeded the bounds of good taste.

Following Colorado's 27-21 victory over Nebraska on Nov. 4, the Omaha *World-Herald* editorialized that the Buffaloes were trying "to hype his death into a sort of '12th-man' presence on the Colorado team."

The newspaper referred to Aunese's "secular canonization - St. Sal, as it were," and said his locker had been "turned into the kind of shrine that is sometimes seen in the great cathedrals of Europe. Aunese's helmet and jersey on view the way the relics of Christian saints are displayed in the Old Country."

McCartney, although admitting he had been distressed by the vehemence of the World-Herald editorial, observed: "I don't be-grudge anybody on the outside that finds fault or takes exception to what's been going on here. It's really been quite authentic, genuine, spontaneous. Nothing's been orchestrated or planned, and it continues to happen. Nobody knows what's next.

"At the senior banquet, each player had an opportunity to talk about his football experiences. Every one of them got up and talk-ed about his relationship with Sal. They hadn't talked it over. They were talking from the heart. And we don't have to try to explain it. It's real. It's bona fide."

McCartney could understandably have been embittered by Aunese's having fathered his daughter's child. Instead, he prayed with Aunese in his hospital room shortly before Sal's death.

"I'm so grateful that our daughter was strong enough to go through with this because now we have this precious child in our home who's so full of life," McCartney said. "He's a very active baby, frisky. Much like his old man. When he grows up I'll tell him that his dad was a team guy, unselfish, a hard worker, very loyal, very wholehearted. Timothy's got big shoes to fill."

(December 24, 1989)

∼ Colorado fell one win short of Sal Aunese's Orange Bowl dream, losing 21-6 to Notre Dame on Jan. 1, 1990. One year later the Buffaloes defeated Notre Dame 10-9 in the Orange Bowl to win the national championship in The Associated Press poll. Sal Aunese's son, Timothy Chase "T.C." McCartney, grew up to be a quarterback at Louisiana State University. ∼

Thirty-six

Polyester peacocks

A brief chromatic course for the GTE Suncoast Classic at the TPC of Tampa Bay:

The grass is green, the sky is light blue, the water is dark blue, the jasmine is yellow and the heather is purple.

And the golfers' clothes are green, light blue, dark blue, yellow, purple, red, orange, fuchsia, chartreuse, puce, aquamarine, burnt umber ... and that doesn't even include Doug Sanders' outfit.

Tommy Bolt, no shrinking violet, once said of Sanders: "The man looks like a jukebox with feet. In fact, even his feet look like jukeboxes."

What is it with golfers that causes them to dress as if they had been caught in an explosion at the Crayola factory?

"Golfers want to be different," Larry Mowry explains. "We're a bunch of individuals, anyway ... this isn't a team sport ... and the bottom line is, some guys, their personality says, 'Hey, look at me.' "

Anything else?

"Yeah," Mowry adds. "They can't lose you in the woods."

Chi Chi Rodriguez has a more down-to-earth reason. "I had one pair of pants, blue jeans, when I was a kid. When they tore, my mother put a patch on them. I worked all my life to get out of blue jeans. That's why I dress flashy."

But why red?

"So the TV cameras can find me in the woods."

Are we finding a common thread here?

The truth of the matter is that it's downright hard to look bad on a golf course. You can dress like a clown and have people ask where you shop. - **author Lewis Grizzard**

"Guys may dress conservatively the rest of the time," says Billy Casper, who favors neon-bright plus fours (knickers) that highlight his corpulent frame. "When they get out on the golf course, because it is a completely different area, they relax and have fun and like to wear colorful clothing. Maybe to attract attention. To give the people a smile."

Why should the people smile at Sanders, Casper and their ilk when the people look more like golfers than the golfers?

Why do otherwise normal, austere businessmen (women are not excluded, but their innate sense of good taste and common sense keeps their participation to a minimum), who drive Academy Gray Cadillacs and wear charcoal gray suits, suddenly appear in public in mix-and-match plaids, checks and stripes, in fluorescent pants dotted with tiny flamingos, pelicans, alligators, turtles or sea gulls?

"It must have something to do with genetics," Jim Colbert offers, "that they want to do something they can't do in the office and they can't walk down a New York City street in. So when they come to the golf course they go nuts. They put on everything they don't have the guts to wear anywhere else."

Do guide dogs select their raiments?

Well, close.

"When I get up, if it's not dark, I have a better shot at it," NFL quarterback-turned-Senior Tour golfer John Brodie says, explaining why, on this particular day, his lemon-yellow sweater and lime-green slacks actually make a rather attractive combination. "If it's dark, whatever I end up with, that's it."

If he is winging it with his wardrobe ... the smile suggests he isn't ... Brodie is at one end of the haberdashery spectrum, the elegant Casper at the other. "I have eight outfits with me," Casper says, "and I'll flop back and forth among them. People wait to see what I'm going to wear the next day."

At the 1983 U.S. Senior Open at Hazeltine, Casper and Rod Funseth were tied after four rounds, forcing an 18-hole playoff. "The first question," Casper recalls, "was, 'Do you have anything to wear tomorrow?' I told them what I had and allowed them to select what I'd wear. It was a pink pair of pants and a cherry shirt with matching argyle socks."

Casper won.

"*Golf is not a sport. Golf is men in ugly pants walking.*" - Comedian Rosie O'Donnell

"Yeah, I've seen a lot of ugly people in ugly pants walking," says Lee Trevino. He admits that he is not entirely blameless. In 1968, he attended an end-of-the-tour dinner. It was his first visit to New York. "I went up there with summer pants on, orange ones," Trevino says. "They were actually whistling at me when I walked down the street."

If he has ever gotten heat for his choice of attire, he won't admit it. "My caddie weighs 310 pounds," Trevino says of Herman Mitchell. "Nobody gives me any heat about anything."

Some of his compatriots are not so lucky.

"I've gotten ragged for clashing with a golf course," Brodie says.

"I got into a purple thing in '87," Mowry adds. "Seems like everything I wore was a shade of purple. The fans really gave it to me, like, 'Hey, I heard you two holes away.' And a lot of Minnesota Vikings stuff."

Of late, Mowry has been eschewing the more colorful garb. "I'm not playing as well as I used to," he says, "so I'm not as flashy with the dress. I want to blend in, not be seen so much."

Once upon a time, Groucho and Chico Marx were playing Hillcrest Country Club at Beverly Hills. Because of the heat, they decided to remove their shirts. They were reprimanded by an official who pointed out that club rules required shirts at all times.

The next time they teed off, they wore shirts … and no pants. "Where does it say members must wear pants?" Groucho inquired.

The rule book was immediately revised.

At Hillcrest, shirts and pants are now required.

Taste is optional.

(February 13, 1992)

As the years have passed, most golfers (the professionals, anyway) have toned down their attire. Then there's John Daly …

Thirty-seven

Hands of greatness

ATLANTA - It's going to hurt when she scrubs. It always does. The antiseptic stings the abrasions on the wrists, arms and elbows of Dorothy Richardson, M.D.

"Yeah, I know, and I keep saying to myself, 'Dot, you've got to stop sliding headfirst,'" she says, stripping off her Windbreaker and displaying a welter of green-and-purple bruises and red, rough skin, the residue of occasional belly-flop slides into the base of her choice.

Is this any way for an orthopedic surgeon in the making to treat her hands … two of her most valuable assets?

"I can't help it," she says. "This is the only way I know to go."

Full bore. That's been her speed since … well, as Joyce Richardson, her mother, says, "She was born at high speed. She ran before she ever walked. She doesn't ever slow down. She's either going all-out or she's asleep."

One more year

Dot Richardson could be a juggler, the way she runs her life. Fact is, she is. On the one hand, a budding medical career; on the other, playing softball better than any other woman in America, if not the world.

Most future physicians have their hands full just with their studies. To interns and residents, with their brain-bending hours and marathon sessions in the hospital, staying awake and alert becomes a profession in itself.

Richardson shrugs at the observation. She can't count the times she has rushed from an operating theater, torn off her surgical gloves and gown and traded them for a glove and double-knits and taken the field an inning or two into a game.

"Not that it gets any easier," she says. "It doesn't. But I take life a day at a time. And I catch some sleep whenever I can."

Truth be told, she's been playing it a year at a time.

When she received her master's degree in exercise physiology from Adelphi University in New York, she thought she had played in her last World Championships, her last Pan Am Games.

She was ready to say, 'That's it. It's been a good run, but it's time to move on.' Three-time batting champion at UCLA, four-time All-American, NCAA Player of the Decade for the '80s. What was left?

Well, there was the Olympics. But that was a fantasy anyway. There was medical school. That would be her life.

Except the medical staff at Louisville encouraged Richardson to play ball. Okay, she said. One more year.

"I've been doing 'one more year' for eight years now," she said.

'Who's going to get it?'

Richardson was an Air Force brat, the fourth of Ken and Joyce's five children, raised on military bases in Guam, England and all over the United States.

"Remember the time," Joyce said, smiling at her husband, "when she was, like, a year old or so? She lived in Guam from nine months to a year and a half. There was this 10-foot fence by the house where there was this drop-off for drainage into the ocean, and you could see her on the top of that fence at that age, like some kid trying to climb out of her crib.

"She was something," her mother said. "Wore the rubber right off a tricycle."

One of her brothers, Kenny, three years older, was the star athlete at Colonial High School in Orlando. All-everything. Most Valuable Athlete in the school his senior year. Then came Dot.

She played basketball, fast-pitch and slow-pitch softball, tennis, volleyball. She ran track. And in every one she was all-conference.

"The awards banquet her senior year, they had a real problem," her father said. "The Most Valuable Athlete had always been a boy, and they had another good one that year, a football player. And here was Dot. We're sitting at the table and there's all this talk, 'Who's going to get it?'

"They decided they'd better have two of 'em. They still do, one for the boys, one for the girls. But our Dot, she started it."

'What would I have become?'

It started a lot earlier for Richardson. Seventh grade was something of a turning point. She had played baseball before that. Pickup games, nothing organized.

"This was 22, 23 years ago," her mother said. "Girls didn't do that then; not much anyhow."

She ran track on the boys team. But they turned her down for baseball. Richardson's eyes seemed to harden just slightly at the memory.

"What am I supposed to do about that?" she said. "If I couldn't throw hard enough or run fast enough or hit the ball, okay, I could accept that. But when it's because you're a girl ..."

All that was left was softball. She had played slow-pitch and fast-pitch on and off since age 10. The day her school turned her down for baseball, she found a women's team for which she could play. The average age was 22. Richardson was 12, maybe 13. The women on the team had a problem with her. Don't throw the ball so hard to first, they said.

A lot of her friends in high school gave up sports. It wasn't worth fighting society, Richardson said. "They quit because they weren't getting the dates they wanted. They were getting stereotyped, that wanting-to-be-a-man stuff, and they couldn't deal with it. Now I get calls from them: 'What would I have become?'"

Elbows

The break between her first and second years in medical school at Louisville was like regular college, Richardson said … a 2½-month stretch when she could play a summer softball season.

Her second year, the school did a lot of schedule-swapping to keep her playing. She worked during the week and played on weekends. Year by year, she kept going. After medical school, she decided, that's when she would quit.

During her fourth year, she put together her match list. The students, having visited prospective hospitals and schools where they might go through residency, list them in order of preference. The hospitals and schools have their lists, ranking students.

Richardson wanted Southern Cal. It wanted her. Done. Of course, she realized, this really would be it for softball.

But the university and Los Angeles County Hospital weren't ready to take away her dream. She always wanted to play softball in the Olympics. She even turned down a chance to play in a pro league in 1977 … 15 years before softball became a demonstration sport at Barcelona … when she was barely 16; she didn't want to jeopardize her amateur status.

The day she turned in her match list in 1993, softball became an Olympic sport. USC, like Louisville before it, helped her manage medicine and sports. After the second year of a five-year residency, with Richardson hoping to make the Olympic team, the university gave her a year off.

Her third year of residency began July 1, so Richardson took a month's vacation. The medal games are today. Dot Richardson will be at shortstop. If she's lucky she will be scraping up her arms sliding headfirst. On Thursday, Dorothy Richardson, M.D., will be up to her elbows in patients.

(July 30, 1996)

~ Dot Richardson hit the game-winning home run in the gold-medal game at the 1996 Atlanta Olympics and was on the gold-medal team at the 2000 Sydney Olympics. She is an orthopedic surgeon in Florida. ~

Thirty-eight

Emma Culpepper raised a good man

Train up a child in the way he should go; and when he is old, he will not depart from it.- **Proverbs 22:6.**

OCALA - The rear of the L-shaped living room is a veritable shrine to Daunte Culpepper. A glass frame encases the No. 8 jersey he wore for the Fighting Knights of Vanguard High before he graduated and the number was retired. Dozens of trophies, plaques, photos and posters cover walls and shelves, honoring the senior at the University of Central Florida, arguably one of the best college quarterbacks in the country.

In another corner are assembled photos of Daunte and the 14 other children Emma Culpepper raised here. He was the last, reared with the same iron hand ... and leather belt ... that she used on the rest of them.

At the moment, Emma Culpepper sits in the armchair closest to the television, feigning anger. "That Daunte," she says, "what's wrong with that boy? I ought to tan him." Daunte has forgotten to tell her he was the subject of a TV program, and she has missed it.

Whatever excuse Daunte has, it will not be good enough, and he knows it. Emma's word is law. Always has been.

"She was a big disciplinarian," he says during a break in practice at UCF in Orlando. "She'd put the belt on me when I needed it, and I needed it a lot. Not for bad things. I didn't have to be brought home by the police. I never talked back. Small things, like she'd tell me to do the dishes before I went to play and I'd forget and be outside, and here she comes with the belt."

"Oh, my, yes," Emma confirms with a cackle. "Lazy. Very lazy. He wouldn't half do his work. He hated cleaning the yard and washing dishes and stuff like that. I'd have to tan his butt a little bit, then I'd feel sorry. But I wouldn't let him know."

"Looking back on it," Daunte says, "I appreciate everything she did for me, especially the discipline. If she hadn't handled me that way, I never would have turned out the way I did."

'Don't give them away'

Emma Culpepper is 83 and still taking care of herself and Gal, "my guard dog," a small, shaggy, black 4-year-old of indeterminate ancestry. "I get lazy sometimes," she says, "don't feel like cooking." A daughter is always around, or close enough to come by and make dinner.

Emma needs a cane to get around, but when she goes to Daunte's games at the Florida Citrus Bowl or others within driving distance (she's afraid to fly), she is treated like royalty, attended to by 25 or 30 of her family.

It is appropriate for this Queen Mother who not only raised her son right but, without actually saying it, made sure he went to Central Florida, 70 miles from home.

She and her late husband, John Will Culpepper, had no children. But when her brother Hudson was mortally injured in a mill accident, "he asked me on his deathbed to take his four boys and raise them," Emma says. "He begged me, 'Don't give them away. Don't split up my children. Give them all the education you can. They're going to have to be the head of the family.' The oldest was going on 6. I was in my 20s."

Emma and J.W. raised Hudson's children, "and when his wife went to having more kids - she was unmarried, so she depended on me - I took them in, one after the other. After a while there were 12 kids," although she thinks that never more than eight or nine were in the house at a time. "They didn't have nowhere else to go," she says. "I wasn't going to let them run loose in the streets."

J.W. died in an auto accident in 1956. Emma - for years house-mother at the McPherson School for Girls, a home for unwed mothers in Ocala - became mother and father to her brood.

And when some of the children had children of their own, they, too, ended up under her care in the nondescript one-story, three-bed-room, white stucco house. "'The Orphan House' they called it," she says.

There wasn't much money - Emma supplemented her income working as a beautician and doing stoop labor - but there was enough for her and the children to get by. She put food on the table and clothes on their backs. They were all kin, and "they didn't give me a lot of headaches. These children were so mannerable. You know what the Bible says; train your children right when they're young and they'll do right later on."

They are anywhere from their 20s to their 60s now - teachers, sec-retaries, dietitians, laborers, operators of small businesses. Nobody is in trouble with the law. Two of the children's children have children. Emma Culpepper is a great-grandmother.

"The most fulfilling thing in my life is my children," she says. "I love them all, pray for them every day. I don't put Daunte ahead of none of them, and I don't put none of them ahead of God."

'In my mind, she had me'

Emma was 61 when she met Barbara Henderson, a teenager in her charge at McPherson. "Bobby fell in love with me, got to calling me 'Mama,' " Emma says. "She went home to Miami, got in some more trouble (sentenced to five years in jail for armed robbery) and started calling me, begging, 'Please take my baby.'

"I said I couldn't. I was getting up at 3 in the morning to be at work by 6. How was I going to raise a baby? But Bobby was smart. She kept at it, told me how the state was going to take her baby away, then wrote to her lawyer that I would take the baby. I didn't know anything about it. Then the lawyer called me. I couldn't let her down."

Daunte Culpepper was born Jan. 28, 1977, about a month after Emma's 62nd birthday. When he was 1 day old, Emma took him in. Three years later she adopted him.

"My biological mom came into my life when I was real young," Daunte says. ("I taught him to love his mother," Emma says, "told him, 'If it hadn't been for Barbara, you wouldn't be here. Always respect your mother.' ")

"I knew Emma wasn't my real mother, but I didn't care," he says. "I loved her like she was my biological mom, and she loved me as though I was her own. In my mind, she had me."

He speaks to Barbara on occasion. She stays out of Daunte's limelight. "She's a social worker, a really great woman," he says. "She grew up and was able to bounce back from childhood mistakes."

He doesn't know who his father is. Emma says she doesn't, either. "I don't think about it much," Daunte says. "I've gone this long without one, I don't really need one now, and I had everything I needed growing up. By the time I was going to school, Mom was retired, so she was there every day for me when I got home. That's all she did; she raised me."

Daunte Culpepper and Kimberly Rhem, his high school sweetheart, have a daughter, 18-month-old Lyric. He sees his daughter every weekend. "I told myself a long time ago that if I ever had a kid, I'd try to be the best dad in the world," he says. "Not having a dad, I know what it feels growing up without one."

He says he and Rhem likely will marry but that they're not quite ready. Emma, too, would like to see Daunte take his time.

"He's not settled, don't know nothing about married life," she says. "He's not going to stay home. I'd rather he stay just like this for a while."

'I should be loyal'

Daunte Culpepper grew up with Travis, Lamont and Wayne, older cousins by 11 years or more "who might as well have been brothers," he says. "We slept in bunk beds in the same room every night. We were pretty happy all the time, fighting and arguing. That's what boys do. I was always bigger than anyone my age, so I didn't get picked on much at school. But I was the baby at home. I got it all the time. I think my competitive nature came from living with those guys."

When he was 12, he was playing city-league football, and he was a wide receiver. "I thought it was the easiest way to score touchdowns," he says. One day the quarterback overthrew the post pattern he was running in practice. The ball rolled to a stop about 30 yards downfield. Daunte picked it up and slung it back.

The coach caught it, looked at me, threw it to me and said, 'Do that again.' So I threw it back again. From that day on, I was a quarterback."

He was not the best of students. "Hated to study," Emma says. "I'd tell him, 'You're getting A's and B's in basketball and football and C's and D's and sometimes F's in the other things. You ain't going to be able to make it, baby.' "

As a junior at Vanguard he was a recruit highly prized by many major colleges - Florida, Florida State, Miami, Auburn, Clemson and South Carolina, and that's just in the South.

"He's got shoe boxes full of mail," Emma says.

Then the schools got a look at his poor grades and backed off.

But Paul Lounsberry, then UCF's offensive line coach and now offensive coordinator, did not. "He would come here," Emma says, "and make lists of things Daunte had to do to bring his grades up. He pulled Daunte through."

In his first semester as a senior, Daunte's grades rose dramatically. The big-school coaches came back.

Why, they asked him, would he want to go to a little school like UCF instead of a national power?

Daunte remembered what Emma had taught him about loyalty. On national signing day, he committed to UCF.

"Nobody but Coach Lounsberry thought I could make it," he says. "He told me if I just disciplined myself, I could do it. UCF stuck with me the whole way when I really needed them, and when I became eligible, I felt since they were loyal to me, I should be loyal to them."

After three seasons, the past two in Division I-A after UCF made the jump to big-time football, Daunte Culpepper was considered a potential high NFL draft choice, not unlike Steve McNair, selected in 1995 by the Oilers in the first round out of obscure Alcorn State. Millions of dollars awaited Culpepper if he turned pro.

"I talked to my mom and some other people about it," he says. "I thought about it a lot and decided UCF needed me more than the NFL needed me."

'She deserves nicer'

The phone on the floor beside the recliner has rung perhaps half a dozen times in the past hour, a few calls from Emma Culpepper's children or friends, a few from newspapers or magazines requesting interviews.

"Why do you want to talk to me?" she says, both to a visitor and, several times, into the receiver. But she gladly suffers the attention. And being fairly new to all this, she says whatever is on her mind.

The afternoon sun is spilling in. The window air conditioner is fighting a holding action against the heat, and a fan pushes the air around.

Emma Culpepper has lived here 57 years.

"It's an old house, and I know there are a lot of memories in it, but she deserves nicer, and sometimes it's time to move on," Daunte says. "She's been taking care of people her whole life, and maybe it's time for her to be taken care of."

Emma appreciates the thought and will move into a new house, she says, but not if it means losing this one.

"I could leave this house, leave it with a smile, as long as I know it's being taken care of. He don't have to tear this one down. If he wants to tear it down, that'll hurt me. There's a bunch of children would be glad to live here."

(September 30, 1998)

Emma Culpepper was 92 when she died of Alzheimer's Disease on May 5, 2007. Daunte Culpepper was selected by Minnesota in the first round of the 1999 National Football League draft. He spent 11 seasons in the NFL, seven with the Vikings.

Thirty-nine

A game, a business, an identity

S'T. PETERSBURG - They are ours now, ours to enjoy. But it is our children who will love them.

To those of us who have left adolescence in the dust, the Tampa Bay Devil Rays, our new baseball team, will never be invested with the emotional energy that defines our daily joy, our rage, our sadness.

We will grow with them, but we have not grown up with them.

For us, they will never be romance and misty memories, fathers and sons playing catch in the back yard, players in flannel uniforms, on new-mown grass under an azure sky.

Many of us grew up in major-league cities with baseball teams we called our own. If we didn't have a hometown team we adopted one, because we could hear about them over the crackle of the radio, because our brothers wore their caps or because our fathers fulminated about them over dinner.

We knew everything about their players … the way Jackie Robinson danced off third, the way Mel Ott kicked his leg, the number Mickey Mantle wore before he wore No. 7.

We knew all their numbers. We knew their batting averages, even the brand of cigarette they smoked. Ballparks named Crosley, Shibe and Forbes were our shrines.

The ThunderDome will never be a shrine. The players who play in it will never come out of the cornfields of our minds.

We are getting a game. We are getting a business. We are getting an identity.

The children we are raising are nothing like the children we were when baseball seemed somehow more innocent. Our children collect baseball cards not to trade or to clothespin into the spokes of their Schwinns. They collect them as currency, buying them by the boxful and putting them, unopened, on the closet shelf, to mature as a war bond might have when youngsters named Musial, Rizzuto and Stanky were starting to make names for themselves.

But our children will live and die with the next generation of Devil Rays. For our children, the Rays will always have been here.

Our children will remember the first school of Rays as fondly as we remember everyone from Aaron to Zernial because they will grow up with them … even if only briefly in this era of free agency … the way we grew up with Cronin and Clemente, Mays and Marquard, Spahn and Sain (and prayed for rain).

(March 10, 1995)

~ The Thunder Dome (originally the Florida Suncoast Dome), was renamed Tropicana Field in 1996 when Tampa Bay was awarded a Major League franchise. The Tampa Bay Devil Rays played their inaugural game on March 31, 1998. For nine of their first 10 seasons they finished last in the five-team American League East Division and fourth once, in 2004. The team's name was changed to the Tampa Bay Rays in 2008. That season the Rays finished first in the American League East, defeated the Chicago White Sox in the division series and the Boston Red Sox to win the American League championship before losing the World Series in five games to the Philadelphia Phillies. ~

Forty

Life in the last league

S T. PETERSBURG - Ever since he was just a little shaver - say, oh, about 62 - Tom Garrett dreamed of playing with the big boys.

That was when he and Shirley first moved to St. Petersburg, back in January 1977. Six months later, the heat got to them and they moved back to Richmond, Va. By then, though, Tom had seen George Bakewell - just a kid himself then, a stripling of 85 - and the rest of the Kids & Kubs in person.

And Tom Garrett just knew that someday he would have the honor of wearing the bow tie.

The Garretts moved to St. Petersburg for good in 1989. The next year, the year he turned 75, he tied on that tie. It remains a badge of honor.

"I first read about the Kids & Kubs in the '50s, in Richmond, when I was with the postal service," said Garrett, who then was running the softball gamut - church leagues, intercity leagues. "I made up my mind, as the years progressed, that if I ever came here - if I ever lasted long enough - I'd go see the Kids & Kubs and maybe even try to make the team."

As he approached his 75th birthday, he stopped to watch the Kids & Kubs practice just before their 1990 season. "Fortunately," he recalled, "they needed an umpire. I started umping for them, did it for about three months. I was so bad, they finally took me on the team. I guess they figured it was better to have me with them than against them."

Today, Tom Garrett is a catcher and vice president of the Kids & Kubs.

'The uniform is our trademark'

If tradition counts for anything in an era of double-knits, domes and designated hitters, it is the bow tie, that little piece of cloth just south of the jowls of these gentlemen who, for close to five months each year, three days a week, call North Shore Park home (and first, second and third base, too).

Some of the players just as soon would do away with the bow tie, a charming anachronism.

"I've never quite cared for the uniform, the bow ties," said John Veleber, a member since 1988 and captain of the Kubs team. "It's hard, playing in the hot sun, with that thing stuck under your neck."

Do not expect the Kids & Kubs to retire the ties anytime soon. Not if Garrett has anything to say about it - which, of course, he does.

"The ties are part of our uniform, and the uniform is our trademark," he growls good-naturedly. "As long as I'm on the club, I will fight tooth and nail to keep it like it is."

The Kids & Kubs were born in 1930 as the Three Quarter Century Softball Club. Evelyn Barton Rittenhouse was the midwife. She was a Broadway actor who fell in love with St. Petersburg while visiting her mother. Eventually, she moved to the city.

She worked at the Chamber of Commerce and discovered how lonely the elderly could be. They would call, asking about a club for their age group, or their favorite sport. She began organizing clubs for them … the Kids & Kubs, the Show Biz Club …

And when critics complained that the elderly received too much attention, Rittenhouse fired back: "Don't pick on the old people here. We wouldn't have this fine city of today without them."

The Kids & Kubs have outlived Webb's City, Central Plaza and the green benches of downtown St. Petersburg. But what was once so much of St. Petersburg's identity is itself becoming more and more an anachronism as the city becomes more youthful and its citizens and attractions more diverse.

Twenty years ago, when St. Petersburg was known as "God's Waiting Room," there were a lot more seniors to watch the seniors. "There'd be 10 times as many people watching these games - 1,000, 2,000 people," Garrett said. "We've got pictures of it.

"A lot of them didn't have much more to do than come see this team. Most of them didn't have televisions, just radios. Now there's cable (TV), exercise classes, bus tours, cruises. There's something on the calendar for almost every day."

'Like dogs chasing cars'

A few times a month, Michael Schroeder ventures from Largo to Clearwater to spend the weekend with Grandma and Grandpa. He loves computers. He would spend all day in front of one if given the chance.

Arthur and Irene Kelsey don't have a computer. What they have is baseball, softball. He has played ball all his life, and in their 53 years of marriage she almost always has accompanied him to his games.

So when Michael wakes up on a Saturday morning, Grandpa will take him out to the park, jam a glove on his hand and play catch for a while - Kelsey the 75-year-old enthusiastic fielder, Schroeder the 12-year-old willing-if-not-eager partner.

Like the wives of major-leaguers, many of the wives of the players will gather to watch their husbands in action. Unlike the wives of major-leaguers, though, these women do not have to worry about Baseball Annies, women who stalk players with carnal knowledge in mind.

"I don't worry about it because I'm there every minute," Irene Kelsey said. And Shirley Garrett laughed out loud at the thought. "Well, he is pretty good-looking," she said while Tom, her husband of 50 years, smiled winsomely. "I wouldn't object. I mean, it's like dogs chasing cars. What would they do with 'em if they caught 'em?"

What, indeed. Romance is not solely for the young.

About 10 years ago, 71-year-old Eleanor Curley of Waltham, Mass., seven years a widow, visited St. Petersburg. She met 76-year-old Walter Brooks, a widower. He took Eleanor to a minor-league baseball game at Al Lang Stadium. That was nice. Then he took her to a Kids & Kubs game. He was playing in it.

"Oh, my," Eleanor recalled. "The sparks just flew. I love baseball. I think that's when I fell in love with him. I haven't stopped going since."

He stopped playing last year but is still the team chaplain.

On Sept. 26, Walter and Eleanor Brooks celebrated their sixth wedding anniversary. A photograph shows them leaving the church under a canopy of crossed bats held by his teammates.

Two days after the wedding they flew to Sacramento, Calif., where the Kids & Kubs were to play some road games. "A honeymoon with 52 chaperones," Eleanor said.

'You have to be a gentleman'

When Arthur Kelsey wasn't busy as a yardmaster for the Milwaukee Railroad back in Davenport, Iowa, he would pitch semipro baseball. Then he hurt his shoulder and switched to fast-pitch softball. "There's things I can't do overhand anymore that I can still do underhanded, mainly pitch," he said.

This year, the Kelseys' 13th in Florida, he will pitch for the Kids & Kubs. Kelsey will be a rookie. "Made it to the majors," he said with a laugh. "Hey, I made it to the age. That's the real kick."

For years he played in the "minors," in the 3-Score Slo-Pitch Softball League in Clearwater. "Really, it's just a continuation of what I've been doing for 10 years. The only thing is, now there's a bunch of guys older'n me instead of the other way around."

John and Ruth Veleber arrived from Garfield, N.J., 20 years ago, after the rubber mill where he worked for 42 years went bankrupt, "and started counting the years until I could play" for the Kids & Kubs.

As he watched them, he realized that it was more a social club than a ballclub. As Paul B. Good, the Kids & Kubs president, acknowledged: "Ten years ago or so, there were only one or two good players on each team; the rest of them were just, well, old guys."

But as the old guys got younger in body and spirit, the competitiveness changed. Making the Kids & Kubs is no longer a certainty. Candidates are given the once-over by a few veteran players in tryouts - character is as much a factor as ability - and those that pass muster are put on probation for a year.

After that, permanent membership is bestowed "unless you do something to bring shame on the team," Garrett said. But, unlike their millionaire counterparts in Major League Baseball, no member of the Kids & Kubs has been discovered doing drugs ... except for the usual. Dyazide, Procardia, Mevacor ...

"It's not real hard to make the team," Garrett said, "but you have to be a fairly good ballplayer and, above all, you have to be a gentleman. Those two things go hand in glove."

Especially on the ballfield. In the major leagues, the trash talk among players tends toward genealogy. Among the Kids & Kubs, the jibes lean more toward gerontology. "Get the piano off your back" and "I see you found your golf swing again" are old standards.

There are 12 players on the field - five infielders, five outfielders, a pitcher and a catcher. There are no roster limits, but not everyone shows up for every game. Usually, there will be four or five extra players on each bench.

The games don't count, in the sense that there are no standings. "We're playing for fun," Garrett said. And the team captains, Veleber (Kubs) and Harry Shironaka (Kids) try to play as many players as possible. "But if the score is 1-1, 3-2, something like that, the captain's probably going to keep his best players out there. Everyone wants to win."

'He died in my arms'

The competitiveness, the athleticism, has created something of a division in the ranks.

"What takes away from some of the fun," Veleber said, "is that some of the older fellows don't want to give up. They fall flat on their face and it makes the rest of us look bad. I think we should have two clubs. As the fellows get older, I think there should be a separate team for them."

They tried it last year, forming two more teams, the second pair playing after the first. But most players wanted nothing to do with a demotion (if that's what it was) to the second team.

"They'd say, 'Oh, I'm still good enough,' " Veleber said, "even if they were getting one hit a year. Some of them understand that they can't do it anymore and retire, and some are willing to practice and then just sit out the games. But a few get angry when you try to tell them to take it easy."

It is understandable. No one wants to be told it is time to step aside and make room for someone younger. Not a 37-year-old in the majors, not a 77-year-old in St. Petersburg.

"Resentment, that's just human nature," Garrett said. "Everyone who shows up in uniform feels, 'I can play just as well as that guy.' Maybe physically he can't do it. But in his mind, he can. I'll tell you one thing: Every one of us, when we stand at the plate and look out at the field, in our mind's eyes, it's 20, 30, 40 years ago. We're not seeing a bunch of old men."

A moment later, though, Garrett grinned and said: "The first thing I learned is that when you walk up to a player, don't say, 'How do you feel?' Because he'll tell you. And it'll take forever."

The reality is that some of the Kids & Kubs have undergone hip replacements and triple-bypass heart surgery. Time is their enemy.

"In baseball," Garrett said, "a player gets hurt, he may not be able to play anymore, but he's got a life to get on with. Here, someone gets hurt …"

These men, for all their youthfulness, are very aware of their mortality. They are all too painfully reminded of it periodically.

On a sunny June day in 1992, Garrett and 81-year-old George Icke Jr., were on the field at North Shore Park. Icke was in charge of producing the club's annual brochure. "He was very proud of it," Garrett said. "He knew it was going to be printed that day. He turned to me and said, "Tell 'em the presses start in five minutes.' I turned to catch a ball and turned back to say something to him, and he was gone."

Just a few months earlier, Veleber was sitting in the dugout next to Irvin Holzhueter, a 76-year-old pitcher. "He'd just come off the mound, and we were talking and the next thing, he sort of leaned up against me," Veleber said. "He died in my arms."

And Garrett added: "We all think about it, sure. We know it's got to happen eventually. And there isn't a man on this club, that if he had to go, he'd just as soon go right on that field."

(October 27, 1993)

Forty-one

Daybreak at the races

OLDSMAR, Fla. - This is where the dreams begin, in virtual dark-ness, in the cool morning air, in a Spartan stable.

It is well before dawn and it is far from the finish line, the grand-stand and the pari-mutuel windows, where dreams of a different sort live and die a thousand times a day.

This is the backside, behind the backstretch fence, where an in-vestment of a few thousand dollars, a flier on a half-ton of horseflesh, can give birth to lucrative trips to the winner's circle or a very expen-sive pet.

The pungent smell of straw, soap, rubbing alcohol and horse is ev-erywhere.

Like the wings of a theater where scenery is taken out of storage, where actors rehearse their lines long before the curtain rises and the spotlight hits the stage, this is where and how a Tampa Bay Downs day begins.

A groom mucks out a stable. Next door, a horse stands by idly while a blanket and saddle are laid across his back and a girth cinched under his belly.

He glances back occasionally, looking at the young woman who keeps up a non-stop stream of conversation with her equine friend.

They know each other well, this ash-blond woman in jeans and this chestnut colt with his legs taped above the fetlock, protecting the cannon bone.

They know each other's moods and habits. He will give an occasional grunt or wuffle.

This one won't bite or kick unless really provoked, not like one a few doors down that will chase her out of the stable just for kicks.

Maybe the horse won't work out in the morning.

A horse wants to run. That's his breeding. He can get so high-strung you can see his skin rippling, he wants so badly to run. Let him on the track and he might just take off. But a horse needs his energy.

Run him hard in the morning and he's worthless in the afternoon.

Maybe he'll just walk around the stables. He'll get all dressed up - blankets, saddle, bridle - then the exercise rider will take him around the stables.

If he's going to race that afternoon, there might be a morning workout, a light jog on the track to loosen him up and clear his lungs, like an athlete stretching and warming up before the game. It's a way of telling the horse, "Today you're going to do something."

Whichever horses are leaving the stables, they will be handsome - their bodies brushed, their tails and manes combed, their hooves picked clean, fresh wraps on their legs. No straw, no dirt.

A horse is a reflection of its owner

A horse emerges from the gloom, whizzes by almost silently, then fades back into the fog and darkness. This track is sandy beneath the dirt, easy on the feet.

Marshall Novak, architect and owner/trainer of thoroughbreds, stands by the rail, listening to the rhythmic muffled thud of hooves.

He's been here since 1960, racing horses up and down the East Coast. You might call him a pinhooker, buying a horse for a few thousand dollars, putting some time and more money into it, racing it for a while, then selling it for more. And starting over again.

Novak has eight horses at the moment. He's had more, had less. Some have given him a very nice return on his investment; others, well...

"There's a saying," Novak offers. " 'Where there are yearlings there are no suicides.' "

Walter Nazarenko can tell you about hitting it right.

Awhile back he bought Amber's Problem, a 1983 bay colt. "He didn't look like much. No decent breeding," he said. "Good name, Amber's Problem. He'd been a problem for other guys. I never thought he'd be much, but you never know."

Amber's Problem has started 142 times, according to Triangle Publications, which puts out the Daily Racing Form. Twenty-nine wins, 25 seconds, 19 thirds and $344,859 in winnings.

It's rare you'll see the big-stable owners around the backside. Usually they'll show up with their friends for the races, to bask in the reflected glow from the high-priced horseflesh. But the mom-and-pop stables, the owners are here every morning.

Ruth and Joseph Sciro are the definition of mom and pop. She used to be a service representative for the phone company in Ohio. Now she owns three horses. Joseph trains them. He has always trained horses. That's how she got into it.

Smack Water Jack is in Stall 27. "He got named for a song in a jukebox in a bar in New Jersey," Ruth Sciro says. The 4-year-old gelding has started 27 times in a year and a half. Two firsts, five seconds, three thirds. Lifetime earnings: $23,443. But his last start, at Thistledown, he won. You never know.

A horse new to racing can scare easily. He might work out in the company of other horses. Or, if he has a companion at his stall, he might have one of a number of track ponies for a buddy as well.

A track pony is usually an older horse that will put up with almost anything. You know how the old family dog will tolerate the baby pulling its ears, yanking its tail, playing with its paws. The track pony will get its mane chewed, its neck bitten and it won't care - usually.

If horses are working out at a half-mile, a mile, whatever, they're timed by the clockers. Say 20 horses are going a half-mile. The fastest one will get a bullet next to its name for the tout sheets that bettors peruse.

How important is a bullet workout? Who's to say? Run a 2-year-old with a bunch of 8-year-olds, run with horses of varying quality, and the worth of the numbers is open to discussion.

Mornings are for teaching

Out on the track, a trainer may run his 2-year-old with an older horse. The veteran holds the lead heading into the final turn, then eases up to let the baby go by. It's horse psychology, letting the newcomer know what it's like to win. Running behind all the time, with dirt flying in your face, not to mention another horse's tail, can get discouraging.

Other trainers smile and say this bit of psychology is, well, crazy.

More newcomers may be learning the starting gate. It's a tight squeeze in there, frightening. So the horse is walked into the gate, the front doors are closed so he knows what that's like, then the rear ones are closed.

When the horse gets acclimated, the front doors are opened - no bells or anything - and the horse is walked out. After a few of those, they're opened and the horse runs out. And pretty soon he is approved for the starting gate.

Off comes the tack as soon as the workout ends. If it's chilly, a blanket goes on. The hot-walker will take the horse for a few turns around the stable to get the sweat off, give him a swallow or two of water, then walk him for another half-hour, or hook him up to the motorized walker. Then there's a warm-water shampoo by the groom and more walking until the thoroughbred is dry.

And back to the stable. There's a hay-net there, for munching and for play. You'll see a horse batting it around with his nose. Or knocking around an empty plastic milk jug hanging in the stall. Or licking the leather strap across the entrance.

He's bored. The stall is his home 23 hours a day.

By noon, activity on the backside is winding down, and picking up in the grandstand and at the betting windows.

And they're off!

(December 18, 1996)

Forty-two

Overtime

All I can tell you, 16 years after the fact, is that her name was Barbara, it was my birthday, and the game was about to go into overtime.

I hadn't thought of her in maybe a decade, until about a month ago when the New York Islanders played hockey deep into the night. Suddenly, I could hear her voice once again, delivering one of the great goodbyes of all time.

I had grown up short, fat and Jewish in Bensonhurst, a short, fat and Jewish section of Brooklyn. By the time I had reached puberty, it had seemingly eluded my grasp.

Intimidation was a way of life when it came to relationships with the opposite sex and most of the same sex. I'd listen to my old Woody Allen albums and wonder if he was following me around, taking notes.

It took relocating in Los Angeles in the late '60s to loosen me up. I remember the first Saturday morning in my apartment, one I had hastily rented on a Wednesday afternoon. I worked for The Associated Press then, the 4-to-midnight shift. The sounds of splashing and giggling awakened me that Saturday. I'd been told about the pool when I'd moved in. I hadn't been told where it was. It was under my bedroom window, and it was overflowing with California girls.

I could, I told myself, spend the rest of my life in the apartment. Or I could get on with it. I got on with it.

Within the hour, I had said a hyperventilated hello to someone in a bikini, had gotten a friendly hello back and hadn't died. By Sunday evening, I had decided there might be more to night life than Rowan and Martin, the Smothers Brothers ...

Fast-forward to March 1971. I'd been promoted by The AP to New York the preceding June and my social life had skidded to a crawl, due in part to the lack of a swimming pool in my fifth-floor walkup and to the less relaxed atmosphere of Manhattan. I was rediscovering prime time. Then, Barbara.

A friend told her about me and, when she didn't object, he told me about her.

A little about her. Very little. She lived in a loft in the Village - Greenwich Village to anyone beyond New York's borders - and she was a teacher.

And to a 29-year-old Manhattan sports writer who still saw himself as a short, fat kid from Brooklyn, Barbara was astounding.

We'd spent some time on the phone that first time. By mutual consent, we had decided against describing ourselves. So I was ill-prepared for what opened the door.

She was blonde. She was curves. And she was close to six feet tall - close to half a foot taller than I was. She was the Aryan dream/nightmare come alive.

While we were talking, I was mentally rehearsing "Oh, I understand" lines for the moment she decided something had come up or she'd gotten a headache. Then she said she was ready, she was hungry, and if I liked Italian, she knew this great place ...

Dinner was great. So was the next weekend and the next few after that. Was I falling in love? Probably not, but it *was* nice.

The Rangers were in the Stanley Cup playoffs. I had tickets for Sunday night's game. Normally, I'd have called one of my friends. But now there was Barbara.

Sure, she said. She'd never been to a hockey game. It'd be fun. And because April 29 was my birthday, dinner would be on her. Gallagher's 33, a late, lamented great steakhouse half a block from the Garden - Madison Square Garden to anyone beyond New York's borders.

"What time does the game end?" she asked during the meal, interrupting my explanation of icing.

"About 10, why?"

"I've got to be on a bus at 7 in the morning," she said. "Teachers' conference. Upstate."

After the requisite three periods, the Rangers and Chicago were tied 2-2.

Barbara looked at me.

"Overtime," I said. "As soon as somebody scores, it's over. Doesn't happen very often. Don't worry about it."

After the first 20-minute overtime, it was still 2-2. It was nearly 11 p.m.

"Listen, it's getting late ..." Barbara started.

"Look," I interrupted. "It can't go on much longer." I was sweating.

After the second 20-minute overtime, it was still 2-2. It was approaching midnight.

"I've got to get out of here," Barbara said.

"Wait a minute," I said.

"No. I can't stay anymore. Let's go."

I stared at Barbara.

"Well?"

"Barbara," I pleaded. "Look, this is one of the greatest hockey games in the history of the world. You can't ask me to leave now!"

"I can't stay!"

"You can sleep on the bus."

Barbara stared at me.

"I've got to get out of here."

I stared at Barbara.

"Barbara, You can't do this to me! You're asking me to make a choice. I - I - Barbara, you'll come in second!"

Barbara stared at me. She started to get up.

"I'm sorry. Look, I - here," I said. "Take this. Take a cab. I really wish you wouldn't ..."

Barbara took off.

She probably wasn't even out of the building when Pete Stemkowski scored for the Rangers 89 seconds into the third overtime.

I went home, alone.

Wednesday night. I sat on the edge of the bed, conducting an imaginary phone call. It never lasted more than a couple of seconds. "Oh, get it over with," I muttered.

I dialed.

"Hello?"

"Barbara? It's Bruce."

"Hi.`"

She didn't hang up. Now what?

"How was the conference?``

"Okay."

Don't apologize. Don't apologize.

"Barbara, I'm sorry."

"It's okay."

My God, it's okay! She understands! She knows what the game meant to me.

"You busy this weekend?"

She knew exactly what it meant.

"I'm busy," Barbara said, "for the rest of your life."

(May 27, 1987)

Bruce Lowitt was born in Brooklyn, New York, in 1942 and was a Brooklyn Dodgers fan until sundown on September 29, 1957, after they had played their last game before deserting their fans for Los Angeles. Lowitt began his journalism career in 1965 with the *Daily Item* in Port Chester, New York. He joined The Associated Press in 1967 in Los Angeles (where he ignored the Dodgers as much as possible), and moved to The AP's New York Sports Department in 1970, eventually becoming Pro Football Editor and, later, a national sports features writer covering Super Bowls, World Series, Olympic Games, NBA and college basketball and football championships, the Indianapolis 500 and U.S. Open Tennis. In 1986 he joined the St. Petersburg Times in the same role. He retired from fulltime writing in 2004. Lowitt has appeared on national and local television and radio sport-talk programs, and has written numerous magazine articles and for the Major League Baseball Players Association and AARP websites, and has co-authored several sports books for the youth market. His stories have appeared in *A Century of Champions, The Sports Immortals, The Fireside Book of Baseball* and The Sporting News *Best Sports Stories* anthologies. He and his wife live in Oldsmar, Florida.

Photo by Sandra Plevin

283

Made in the USA
Columbia, SC
07 May 2018